Debating Humanism

Edited by
Dolan Cummings

SOCIETAS

essays in political
& cultural criticism

imprint-academic.com

Published in the UK by Societas
Imprint Academic, PO Box 200, Exeter EX5 5YX, UK

Published in the USA by Societas
Imprint Academic, Philosophy Documentation Center
PO Box 7147, Charlottesville, VA 22906-7147, USA

ISBN 184540 069 0
ISBN-13 9781845400699

A CIP catalogue record for this book is available from the
British Library and US Library of Congress

Contents

Contributors

Josie Appleton is a journalist and writer based in London. She is convenor of the Manifesto Club, writes for *spiked* (www.spiked-online.com), and has contributed to number of other publications, including *The Times*, *Times Literary Supplement*, and the *Spectator*. Her main research focus is looking at the estrangement from our humanity, and how this affects our views of and relationships with animals.

Bob Brecher is reader in philosophy in the School of Historical and Critical Studies, University of Brighton, and director designate of its Centre for Applied Philosophy, Politics and Ethics. He is a former president of the UK Association for Legal and Social Philosophy, and currently a representative of the UK Campaign for the Future of Higher Education. He has been a visiting research fellow in the Centre for Philosophy and Public Affairs at the University of St Andrews, and a visiting research and teaching fellow at the Department of Political Science at the Hebrew University of Jerusalem. His books include *Getting What You Want? A Critique of Liberal Morality*; and *Torture and 'the Ticking Bomb'* will appear in 2007. He is also a consulting editor for *Res Publica* and a member of the editorial board of *Philosophy of Management*.

Simon Blackburn is professor of philosophy at Cambridge University and a fellow of Trinity College. As well as academic works, he has published a number of popular books on philosophy, including an introduction to philosophy, *Think* (1999), and an introduction to ethics, *Being Good*

(2001). He also wrote *Lust* (2004), the *Oxford Dictionary of Philosophy* (1994), *Truth : A Guide for the Perplexed* (2005), and most recently *Plato's 'Republic': A Biography*. He is a fellow of the British Academy, a frequent contributor to *New Republic*, and to discussion programmes on radio. He reviews for the *Independent* and *The Sunday Times*.

Andrew Copson is responsible for education and public affairs at the British Humanist Association, the national membership organisation for humanists and the non-religious. His work focuses on reform of religious education, the abolition of compulsory worship in schools, and the promotion of inclusive and accommodating community schools.

Dolan Cummings (editor) is the editorial and research director at the Institute of Ideas (IoI) and co-convenor of the annual Battle of Ideas festival. He also edits the IoI's reviews website *Culture Wars*, for which he writes about theatre, film and books. He previously edited a collection of essays based on the IoI's 'Ideas, Intellectuals and the Public' conference in 2003 as a special issue of the academic journal CRISPP (vol. 6, no. 4), which is also available as a book, The Changing Role of the Public Intellectual (2005).

Dylan Evans is the author of several popular science books, including *Emotion: The Science of Sentiment* (2001) and *Placebo: The Belief Effect* (2003). After receiving his PhD in philosophy from the London School of Economics, he did postdoctoral research in philosophy at King's College London and in robotics at the University of Bath before moving the University of the West of England (UWE) where he was senior lecturer in intelligent autonomous systems. He left UWE in July 2006 to start the utopia experiment (see www.dylan.org.uk).

Anthony Freeman took degrees in chemistry and then theology at Oxford University. He was ordained in 1972 and held a variety of pastoral and teaching posts in the

Church of England until being dismissed by his bishop for publishing a naturalist account of Christianity, *God In Us: A Case for Christian Humanism* (SCM Press, 1993; 2nd edition Imprint Academic, 2001). He remains a priest and preaches regularly as well as lecturing and writing on theological and consciousness matters. He has been managing editor of the *Journal of Consciousness Studies* since its launch in 1994. His other published works include *Gospel Treasure* (SPCK, 1999) and *Consciousness: A Guide to the Debates* (ABC-Clio, 2003).

Frank Furedi is professor of sociology at University of Kent, and author of a number of books including *Politics of Fear, Where Have All the Intellectuals Gone?*, *Therapy Culture, Paranoid Parenting* and *Culture of Fear*. During the past decade his intellectual work has been devoted to clarifying the meaning of humanism for the twenty-first century. In *Politics of Fear* he argues that the politics of fear thrives in an atmosphere where the exercise of human agency is regarded with suspicion if not dread — and that the alternative to this culture of misanthropy is to set about humanising our existence.

AC Grayling is professor of philosophy at Birkbeck College, University of London, and a supernumerary fellow of St Anne's College. He has written and edited many books on philosophy, including most recently *Among the Dead Cities* and *The Form of Things: Essays on Life, Ideas and Liberty*. He is a regular reviewer and writer for several publications, and a frequent broadcaster on radio. He is the editor of *Online Review London*, and contributing editor of *Prospect* magazine. In addition he sits on the editorial boards of several academic journals, and for nearly ten years was the honorary secretary of the principal British philosophical association, the Aristotelian Society. He is a past chairman of June Fourth, a human rights group concerned with China, and has been involved in UN human rights initiatives. He is a fellow of the World Economic Forum, and a member of its C-100 group on relations between the West and the Islamic world.

Dennis Hayes is joint president of the University and College Union, the largest further and higher education union in the world. He is the head of the Centre for Professional Learning at Canterbury Christ Church University and the author of several books, most recently *The Dangerous Rise of Therapeutic Education: how teaching is becoming therapy* (with Kathryn Ecclestone). He also writes a regular column for FE Focus in the *Times Educational Supplement*.

Elisabeth Lasch-Quinn is an American cultural historian and professor of history at Syracuse University in New York. She is author of *Race Experts: How Racial Etiquette, Sensitivity Training and New Age Therapy Hijacked the Civil Rights Revolution*, in which she traces the evolution of racial discourse in the US from the civil rights movement of the 1960s to today. She is winner of the Berkshire Conference of Women Historians Book Award, and has also written numerous articles and reviews in publications such as the *New Republic*, *Washington Times*, *Encyclopedia of American Cultural and Intellectual History* and the *Journal of Social History*.

Kenan Malik is a writer, lecturer and broadcaster. His main academic interests are in the history of ideas, the history and philosophy of science, race and ethnicity, and theories of human nature. His books include *The Meaning of Race: Race, History and Culture in Western Society* (1996) and *Man, Beast and Zombie: What Science Can and Cannot Tell us about Human Nature* (2000). A new book *Why Do We Still Believe in Race?* is due to be published next year. He has written and presented a number of TV documentaries including *Disunited Kingdom, Are Muslims Hated?*, *Let 'Em All In* and *Britain's Tribal Tensions*. He is also a writer and presenter of Radio 4's *Analysis* programme. An archive of his work can be found at www.kenanmalik.com.

Daphne Patai is professor of Brazilian literature at the University of Massachusetts, Amherst. She is the author and editor of many books, most recently *Theory's Empire: An*

Anthology of Dissent (2005), co-edited with Will H Corral. A former professor of women's studies, Patai has become a critic of the field. She co-authored (with Noretta Koertge) *Professing Feminism: Education and Indoctrination in Women's Studies* (new enlarged edition, 2003), and in 1998 published *Heterophobia: Sexual Harassment and the Future of Feminism. Long concerned about the attack on free speech on American campuses, Patai has been involved with FIRE, the Foundation for Individual Rights in Education, since its inception and currently serves on its board of directors. She is currently at work on a volume of essays entitled 'What Price Utopia?' and Other Essays by a Recovering Feminist.*

Dolan Cummings

Introduction

Debating Humanism

What is a man,
If his chief good and market of his time
Be but to sleep and feed? A beast; no more.

More than to sleep and feed, to be human is to debate, to argue, to think out loud and to engage with the ideas and opinions of others. Over time we have developed countless languages, rituals and technologies to help us do this. And a recurring theme of debate is the very question of what it means to be human, and the nature of our relationship to the world, to each other and to gods or God. This has never been an idle debate: it is intimately bound up with how society is organised and where authority lies. Broadly speaking, the humanist tradition is one in which it is we as human beings who decide for ourselves what is best for us, and are responsible for shaping our own societies. For humanists, then, debate is all the more important, not least at a time when there is much discussion about the unexpected return of religion as a political force determining how we should live.

This collection of essays follows the Institute of Ideas' inaugural Battle of Ideas festival at the Royal College of Art in London in October 2005. Most of the contributors spoke at the festival, and while they discussed a variety of topics, including multiculturalism, the legacy of the Enlightenment, and the place of morality in public life, the question of humanism was never far from the surface. In the essays that follow, the authors deal directly with issues that go to the heart of any debate about where society is going. The question of humanism is about what brings us together as human beings and what we can hope to achieve as such, about the barriers to success and how we might overcome them.

Despite the wider social and political implications of these questions, humanism today is often understood merely as an alternative to religion, a quasi-religious ethic or set of moral principles, but one based on human experience alone rather than God or gods or Providence or any other source of authority beyond this mortal coil. In more political contexts, humanism is often synonymous with atheism, or at least secularism, the idea that faith-based practices and moralism should be kept out of politics. In common parlance, 'I'm a humanist,' usually means simply, 'I don't believe in God.' Those who don't subscribe to any particular religion can opt instead for a 'humanist funeral', for example. Meanwhile, some argue that BBC Radio 4's 'Thought for the Day' slot, which is given over each morning to a representative of one of the various religions, should also have 'humanists' on the roster.

The humanist legacy

There is in fact a long tradition of humanism as a more expansive and meaningful worldview in its own right, rather than simply a godless religion. Historically, humanism in this sense is often identified with the Renaissance, when Europe awoke from the Dark Ages with a renewed interest in knowledge and classical culture and in humanity itself. The term humanist is often used of a particular line of Italian thinkers and writers beginning with Petrarch in the fourteenth century, and also associated with such diverse and colourful figures as the sixteenth century French poet Rabelais and the Dutch scholar Erasmus. These early humanists did not define themselves against religion, though they sometimes found themselves at odds with the church authorities. Rather, they believed positively in the human potential and sought to realise it in their work. More than that, though, the learning, curiosity and richness of spirit exemplified by these figures underpins much of what came after, including not just stunning artistic creativity and intellectual breakthroughs, but religious reform and social and political change too.

It is perhaps in the spirit of humanism to apply an even more generous understanding of the humanist legacy, incorporating the best of human culture from across the globe over the centuries, and reflecting its diversity but also, and perhaps more importantly, its commonality. It is more than just a politically-correct platitude to note that so-called Western civilisation would not be what it is without the contribution of Islamic scholarship, or that ancient Chinese and Indian civilisations made Europe look positively backward in their heydays, and leave us a formidable legacy today. This is not to take an 'all must have prizes' approach to the history of world cultures, however. The fact that for long stretches of time in much of the world nothing much happened makes these occasional flowerings of creativity all the more remarkable. (I am reminded of the comedian Al Murray's joke about the Greeks, who invented democracy, philosophy and classical architecture, and then put their feet up for two thousand years.)

What is striking, however, and what makes civilisation truly *human* rather than specific to particular peoples, is that human beings brought up in any culture can quickly absorb and make their own the best ideas and practices developed anywhere in the world. Think of the current blossoming of Western classical music in East Asia, for example. And such has been the contribution to science in recent years from researchers all over the world that it no longer even makes sense to talk about 'Western science'. Europeans and Americans have been just as quick to assimilate the best art and thought from across the globe, often unwittingly, and certainly without stopping to think if it is compatible with 'Western culture'.

Humanism today

Humanism ought then to mean first of all celebrating the fantastic achievements of humanity, being 'pro-human' rather than 'anti-God'. What makes the question of humanism so interesting and so important today is not simply the putative rise of religion, whether in the form of 'Islamic fundamentalism' in the Middle East and among immigrant communities in the West, or indeed 'Christian fundamentalism' in the USA and elsewhere. Rather, increasing doubt about the supposed inevitability of all societies becoming progressively more secular, rational and modern in the sense in which that term was once understood coincides with a more general uncertainty about the future, and ambivalence about the achievements of humanity. It is perhaps not so much that religion is aggressively attacking otherwise contented secular societies as that those societies have lost faith in the promise of a secular future, and that religion in various forms is rushing in to fill the vacuum.

Debates that take the form of secularism versus religion often reveal unresolved questions within secularism itself. The clearest example is perhaps the banning of Islamic headscarves in French state schools. The French principle of secularism, or *laïcité*, was originally closely wedded to a republican ideal that arguably lacks resonance today *except* in opposition to a politicised Islam. Certainly such a major controversy over the headgear worn by schoolgirls does not speak of a confident and forward-looking secular culture, instead raising doubt about whether individual liberty, religious or otherwise, is compatible with a harmonious society. The ongoing controversy over the teaching of Creationism in the US and Britain meanwhile, has been given an unusual twist by the current prevalence of relativism in Western culture. Creationists argue not that they have the exclusive Truth as revealed by God, but that the scientific theory of evolution is just one theory and that children should be exposed to other ideas too, the better to make up their own minds. In societies in which the authority of science has already been weakened by postmodern ideas, and even Tony Blair is pragmatic about the issue, this is more persuasive than old-fashioned religious dogma. It is opponents of Creationism who often struggle to explain that evolution is more than just another 'faith position'. Finally, serious debate about the 'assisted dying' legislation recently proposed in the UK was inhibited by the widespread belief that opposition to it was necessarily 'faith-based' and therefore beyond rational argument. Consequently a valuable opportunity to discuss society's attitude to death and dying and human dignity was largely missed.

These examples point to the need for more substantial debate about what humanism might and should mean in the future, not simply in opposition to religion and faith-based politics, but as a worldview in its own right.

Several contributors to this volume are members of the British Humanist Association,[1] the national membership organisation for humanists and the non-religious. Two of the contributors, Frank Furedi and Josie Appleton, are currently involved along with myself in setting up the Manifesto Club,[2] a new political initiative based on humanist aspirations rather than the conventional oppositions and formulae of the past. For many of us, then, the questions explored in the collection have a certain urgency, and the opportunity to engage with others, both to make common cause and to identify new points of contention, is invaluable. All of the contributors show an admirable desire to grapple with the challenges facing humanism and to test their own ideas. Humanism is not something to be taken for granted, and it is therefore encouraging to find such an appetite for debating it.

About the essays

The essays are loosely divided into five sections. In the first, the authors explore the idea of 'secularism in crisis', considering the contention that the supposed triumph of secular liberalism over religion and superstition in its various forms masks deeper problems with secularism itself, and

[1]   www.humanism.org.uk
[2]   www.manifestoclub.com

revisiting unresolved questions about the spiritual foundation of modern societies. If secularism is indeed in crisis, is
humanism the solution, and what might that mean? The
remaining essays look at various areas in which such questions have arisen. The second section is on humanism and
religion, the third on humanism and identity, and the fourth
on humanism and education. The fifth section is on the
future of humanism, and explores different conceptions of
what humanism might mean. Simon Blackburn's eloquent
rejection of the transcendental, for example, offers a clear
vision of what humanism could be, but while much of his
argument echoes points made by other contributors to this
volume, it is not ultimately a vision shared by all of them. In
what follows I have drawn out some further points of agreement and disagreement that cut across all five sections.

All of the contributors can be described as humanists, but
it is clear from their essays that humanism is not a single,
uniform worldview. Indeed, both Dylan Evans and Elisabeth Lasch-Quinn (who writes from the Unites States) warn
against 'fundamentalist secularism' or 'secular fundamentalism', whereby atheists settle on a narrowly anti-religious
version of humanism, mirroring the intolerance of the religious extremists they oppose. For Frank Furedi, humanism
that is defined in opposition to religion is a mere caricature:
genuine humanism is necessarily opposed to dogma of any
kind, because it is committed to exploration. Unsurprisingly,
then, there are a range of humanist positions even in relation
to religion, including the Christian humanism advocated
here by Anthony Freeman. While eschewing anything that
could be called 'fundamentalist atheism', AC Grayling
makes the strongest case against religion, arguing that it is
'a hangover from the infancy of mankind', and that religious grounds for morality lack cogency, offering a sense of
definition or closure rather than an intellectually convinc-
ing worldview. Taking a different tack, Evans notes that
religion can still be appreciated much like art even by people who don't believe in its literal truth. Similarly, Simon
Blackburn concedes that an aesthetic attitude to religion
cultivates the subject's ability to think and feel, while regret-

ting that advocates of religion are rarely so generous about secularism. Andrew Copson argues for a 'values-rich' humanism against the idea that a secular view of life is ultimately sterile, suggesting that humanism can have positive content of its own.

Humanism and universalism

In this spirit, Daphne Patai (another American contributor) argues that humanism's universal aspirations are more important than any secular underpinnings. In contrast, Dylan Evans prizes diversity above any such universalism. Thus, the attempt to give positive content to humanism opens another important area of debate. For several contributors, humanism is rooted in our common humanity. Anthony Freeman's Christian humanism begins with the recognition that this common humanity is more important than religious as well as racial identity. Both Kenan Malik and Daphne Patai are critical of 'identity politics' that divide people according to ethnicity or culture. For Patai, what makes identity politics especially galling is that they are based on particular grievances rather than universal standards — one group makes claims on society on the basis of perceived wrongs, logically depending on others to see beyond their own group interests, while disavowing belief in a common humanity that might underpin such magnanimity. For Dylan Evans, in contrast, is it incumbent upon humanists to be sensitive to such claims, rather than engaging in a 'fundamentalist' tit-for-tat between value systems, such as appears to have taken place with the European controversy over cartoons of the prophet Mohammed in early 2006.

There are disagreements even among those unequivocally opposed to identity politics, however. Kenan Malik argues that the problem is ultimately a bogus biological view of racial difference, or an insistence that historic cultural practices should be valued and protected for no other reason than that they are traditional. For Patai, in contrast, it is the postmodern rejection of our common biology in favour of 'the dogma of social constructionism' and constant cultural flux that undermines the idea of universal humanity. For the same reason, Patai is less worried about the 'environmental determinism' discussed by Frank Furedi—the idea that human beings are passively shaped by circumstances—than an overemphasis on human subjectivity that downplays the role of objective reality.

Perhaps part of the problem is the difficulty in identifying a basis for common humanity beyond our basic biological likeness. As Dylan Evans puts it, unlike those who believe in God or some divine order, 'humanists cannot appeal to any objective or absolute basis to legitimise their own sacred values'. It does not follow simply from our biological likeness that we should respect one another's dignity or freedom, for example. Indeed, both Kenan Malik and Elisabeth Lasch-Quinn note that even without the influence of overt identity politics, contemporary culture lacks a sense of commonality, yoking people instead to particular and incommensurable communities with their own values and rules, or alternatively reducing us to distinct demographic types for niche marketing purposes. 'Liberal secularism', or 'universal', 'Enlightenment' values are just that, values for people who believe in that sort of thing, but not compelling for anyone else. Whereas Lasch-Quinn sees this almost consumerist approach to values as part of 'the modern cult of the individual', Malik argues that the privileging of particular identities actually undermines the idea of the individual: 'identity can often seem like the denial of individual agency in the name of cultural authenticity'. For Malik, agency is more important to our humanity than cultural identity. It is the possibility of collective agency that underpins our common humanity.

Simon Blackburn argues along similar lines that we have no need of a supernatural source for 'boundaries to conduct' (or what Dylan Evans calls sacred values), because the source of these is 'in our natures, our needs, our capacities for cooperative action, our sympathies and concerns'. Or as AC Grayling puts it, 'moral striving for a humanist is a matter of trying to understand human nature and the human condition, and on that basis to identify the good for a human being'. Naturally, the question of human nature is crucial to our conception of what humanism might mean, and as the issue of agency implies, this is not merely a biological question. Bob Brecher puts things the other way round, arguing that 'it is political and moral conviction which determine what human nature is taken to be'. Indeed, it is telling that it is Anthony Freeman, making the case for Christian humanism, who is most interested in the science of human nature and philosophy of mind. Far from finding that these undermine Christian belief, as many suppose, Freeman argues compellingly that the latest thinking complements theological thought on the nature of the soul, albeit in a more subtle form than that favoured by Biblical literalists. Brecher's point is not that accounts of human nature shaped by existing convictions are therefore unscientific; a resolutely anti-religious interpretation of the same intellectual developments would be no less 'political'. Rather, it is that Josie Appleton's insistence that, 'All thought and activity should start out from the point of human experience and our desires,' forces us to consider the meaning of those experiences and desires. For Brecher, they are inescapably political because we are fundamentally a political species. Humanism cannot then be non-political, it can only reject existing political formations, which is itself political.

Humanism and politics

Brecher's argument is in part a response to the idea raised by Frank Furedi elsewhere that the current period is best understood as 'pre-political'. Furedi sees the widespread rejection of the idea of progress as a new form of fatalism that frustrates politics. As he argues in this book, 'The reconstitution of agency and historical thinking is the prerequisite for the reengagement of the public with political life'. In a similar vein, Elisabeth Lasch-Quinn writes that 'the notion of a democratic republic involved a sensibility, a disposition, or, one might say, a pre-disposition', perhaps including ideas common to religious and secular traditions, such as 'the belief in the dignity of the human person and in stewardship'. Returning to the question of human nature, then, Josie Appleton's point is to dispute naturalistic accounts of humanity that exclude this predisposition, that is the properly human dimension, by competing 'to find their locus of value as far away from humans as possible', expressing an estrangement from humanity that leads to a disavowal of politics. The question is whether this trend can be challenged in 'pre-political' terms, or whether it requires positive political content such as the socialist humanism proposed by Bob Brecher. Indeed, Kenan Malik argues that the coalescence of left and right around the issue of culture that he describes has been facilitated by the narrowing of politics in recent years, representing an unwelcome accommodation to diminished possibilities.

Similarly, Dennis Hayes sees a diminished view of humanity in what he describes as a dramatic lowering of horizons in education. Both Hayes and Andrew Copson argue that civilisation is transmitted through education, making it a crucial area for anyone interested in the developing humanism, especially if like Copson they want to refute the notion that only 'faith schools' can offer a meaningful framework of values and ethics. Hayes writes that, 'intellectual culture has traditionally been central to our concept of what it is to be human'. What he sees as the displacement of this culture in favour of a model of education based around what is thought to be immediately relevant and accessible to young people thus constitutes for Hayes a de-humanising of education. This too is undoubtedly a political question, but not one addressed in conventional political debates.

All this would seem to reinforce Elisabeth Lasch-Quinn's call for more public intellectual work, interlacing tradition and dissent. As she puts it, while religious fundamentalists' desire to replace science with religion is as undesirable as it is impossible, 'neither can secularists claim to be the party of the future, with so shrunken a moral vision'. Along the same lines, Frank Furedi's call to 'humanise humanism' means recognising and incorporating past failures and mistakes in the humanist legacy. As AC Grayling reminds us, 'human nature itself is too often in unconscious conspiracy with the conscious forces of anti-humanism to thwart them'. Perhaps the human vice to be guarded against most fiercely when it comes to discussing humanism is complacency, the tendency to assume that we have all the answers and that it's the rest of the world that needs to buck up its ideas. That goes as much for those who would smugly dismiss humanism as empty of meaning or historically redundant as those who cling unthinkingly to the banner of humanism as a security blanket against the supposed forces of reaction.

Between them, the essays in this collection move the debate onto new terrain, and show that questions concerning the future of humanism are no more resolved than those thrown up by its legacy. The debate is wide open.

Dylan Evans

Secular Fundamentalism

In its original sense, the term fundamentalism refers to those religious movements that claim to return to the founding principles of their religion, in contrast to the majority of their fellow believers, who the separatists accuse of being corrupt. According to this definition, the phrase 'secular fundamentalism' would be an oxymoron. These days, however, the word is increasingly used in a looser sense, to refer to fanaticism and intolerance of any kind. In this sense, secular fundamentalism has become an unpleasant reality.

My interest in secular fundamentalism began in 2005, after I wrote a short article for the Guardian in which I criticised some fellow atheists, such as Richard Dawkins and Jonathan Miller, for being so hostile to religion (Evans, 2005). Just because one is an atheist, I argued, does not mean that one has to view religion in an entirely negative light. I suggested that atheists could see value in religions by viewing them as works of art—human creations that give wonderful testimony to the remarkable creativity and inventiveness of their creators. Of course they are not literally true—that goes without saying among atheists. But neither is Wagner's Ring cycle literally true, and that doesn't stop me from appreciating its artistic merits.

I did not anticipate the storm of protest that my whimsical little piece would stir up. Within hours of publication, emails started flooding in, and debate started raging on several blogs devoted to atheism and humanism. Most responses were wholly negative. Many were downright rude. In fact, the vitriolic nature of some was eerily reminiscent of the kind of insults levelled at non-believers by religious fanatics, or even the fatwas pronounced by hardline Muslim clerics. In all my life, I had never experienced such a torrent of religious bigotry. And it all came from self-professed atheists. Even Salman Rushdie derided me (Rushdie, 2005). I would have thought that someone like Rushdie, who has been the target of a real and deadly fatwa, might be more open-minded. It was a sorry spectacle, and I confess it almost made me ashamed to call myself an atheist.

Later that year, something happened that proved my concerns about secular fundamentalism to be well founded. In September, the Danish newspaper *Jyllands-Posten* published a series of cartoons, some depicting the founder of the Muslim religion as a terrorist. Many Muslims saw the cartoons as an attack on their faith and culture. In January 2006, the cartoons were reprinted by a Norwegian newspaper, provoking a wave of protests in the Middle East. Saudi Arabia recalled its ambassador to Denmark, Libya closed its embassy in Copenhagen, and gunmen raided the EU's offices in Gaza, demanding an apology. The Danish newspaper apologised, but the next day newspapers in France, Germany, Italy and Spain reprinted the caricatures in solidarity with the Danish and Norwegian press. Angry crowds attacked Danish and Norwegian embassies in Damascus, Lebanese demonstrators set the Danish embassy in Beirut on fire, and five people were killed in protests in Afghanistan. Hundreds of thousands of Muslims joined in further demonstrations in Somalia, Iran, Lebanon, and Malaysia.

Why were the cartoons reprinted in France, Germany, Italy and Spain, when it was clear that millions of Muslims found them extremely offensive? The European newspapers claimed they were defending their right to free speech, but this was disingenuous, since even the most secular countries recognise that free speech is not an absolute, and impose certain restrictions such as prohibiting defamation and incitement to violence. The real issue was not free speech but how sensitive we ought to be to the religious sensibilities of others.

Those newspapers that republished the cartoons were implicitly denying any duty to be sensitive to religious sensibilities, and this is a core trait of secular fundamentalism. Other key aspects of secular fundamentalism include a belief that religion will automatically wither away with the passage of time; an implicit assumption that beliefs are voluntary; and failure to acknowledge the subjective nature of its own sacred values

1. The thesis of inevitable secularisation

Many nineteenth-century thinkers assumed religion would eventually disappear. The gradual process of secularisation would culminate in a world based on science and reason. Today this no longer seems credible. In some societies religion is becoming more important than ever. In the United States and the Middle East religion is resuming the dominant social and moral role it had in Europe before rise of modern science. Even in Europe, we seem to be witnessing the emergence of what the German philosopher Jurgen Habermas has called 'post-secular societies', in which many belief-systems, some religious and some not, compete for followers.

This seems to annoy many humanists and atheists intensely. There seems to be a widespread tendency among people of all creeds and none to think the world would be a better place if everyone agreed with them. Humanists and religious believers alike seem to want to convert the whole world to their own point of view. Yet there seems little prospect of such an eventuality. The world contains a dazzling variety of conflicting and irreconcilable worldviews, and this is probably a permanent feature of human existence. The idea that all rational beings will eventually converge on the same point of view is hopelessly naïve, and only holds good in toy worlds such as that of Bayesian epistemology.

Since diversity of opinion is not likely to disappear any time soon, it would seem rather unhelpful to view it as a

disaster. Besides, as John Rawls has argued, 'to see reasonable pluralism as a disaster is to see the exercise of reason
under the conditions of freedom itself as a disaster' (Rawls,
1995: xxiv), so it is particularly paradoxical for humanists,
who are supposed to value the free exercise of reason, to dis-
parage diversity. Humanists should, rather, view diversity
as a primary good. As a humanist myself, there is nothing—not one single thing—that I wish everyone in the
world would agree about. To my mind, it is the wonderful
diversity of opinion that makes it possible to have such
interesting conversations.

2. The assumption of voluntary credence

The anger some humanists feel towards religious believers
(and which they often deny feeling, despite all the evidence)
also betrays an implicit assumption that people choose their
beliefs. It makes no sense to be angry with someone for
something he is not responsible for, and people cannot be
held responsible for something that they did not freely
choose.

The consensus among most philosophers and psychologists today is that belief formation is a largely spontaneous
and involuntary process. One may choose to investigate or
not investigate a matter, but one cannot choose to adopt a
new belief or reject an old one simply as an act of will. There
can be no such thing, therefore, as an 'ethics of belief', such
that the acceptance of a belief may be judged as ethical or
unethical, or a duty to believe certain things but reject other
things. Many religious traditions concur on this point.
Christianity teaches that faith in god is a gift of the holy
spirit, and the Koran states that there can be no such thing as
compulsion in religion.

It is ironic that religious traditions agree with modern science here, while some humanists do not. Some argue that
we need laws against ridiculing another on the grounds of
his race, but no laws against ridiculing someone on the
grounds of his religious beliefs, because race is not voluntary, while religion is. Even when humanists concede that

religion is not entirely voluntary, they may still be tempted to argue for the same distinction—allowing laws against racial hatred, but ruling out laws against religious hatred—on the grounds that religion is mutable, while race is not. Even if people don't always choose their religious beliefs, they do sometimes come to reject those beliefs after rational debate. But it is hard to see why this consideration should carry much weight. Even if beliefs were entirely voluntary, it would be no more acceptable to stigmatise, marginalise or intimidate people for things they have consciously chosen than for things they have not.

Humanists are begging the question by setting up their own value—that of subjecting of every belief to rational criticism—as the arbiter of the debate. In putting such a high value on rational choice, or at least, rational revision of beliefs, humanists are assuming precisely what many religious believers dispute. For some, religion forms such an integral part of their identity that it would be not merely be painful to stand apart from their beliefs for the purposes of analysis—it would be a subjective disaster. Non-religious people also tend to have such integral beliefs, but they tend to be less willing to acknowledge it.

3. The selective blindness of ethical relativism

Everyone, even atheists and humanists, has what the psychologist Philip Tetlock calls 'sacred values'. Tetlock defines a sacred value as 'any value that a moral community implicitly or explicitly treats as possessing infinite or transcendental significance that precludes comparisons, trade-offs, or indeed any other mingling with bounded or secular values' (Tetlock, 2003). Sacred values need not be taken to have divine sanction, so atheists and agnostics can and do have them too. Common examples of such nonreligious sacred values are racial equality, democracy, justice—and free speech.

Since they do not believe in God, atheists and humanists cannot appeal to any objective or absolute basis to legitimise their own sacred values. They are, in other words, committed to moral relativism. Indeed, this is precisely what lies behind their calls for religious believers not to impose their own religious principles on the rest of society. Yet they often fail to see that this is itself a form of imposition. Take AC Grayling's 2005 new year wish:

> I would like conservatives and fundamentalists in all religions to accept the principles of pluralism and secularism — by the latter meaning a situation in which religious observance is a private affair wholly separated from the public and political domains (Grayling, 2004).

Doesn't Grayling see that this is tantamount to asking religious believers to abandon their religion? An important feature of many religions is that they are not mere private affairs, but make strong claims to regulate the public and political domains. To insist believers leave their religion at the door when they enter the arena of political debate is to assert the sacred values of humanism over the sacred values of religion. It is distinctly anti-pluralist.

There is simply no way round this problem. The secular and religious bases for justifying moral prescriptions are fundamentally different, and there is no reason to think these differences result from the fact that one side is less reasonable or well-informed than the other. The two frameworks are incommensurable; they do not have enough in common, in terms of either shared concepts or shared standards, to resolve their differences, and there is no impartial third standpoint, accessible to any reasonable and well-informed person, that could be invoked to resolve the conflict.

As Slavoj Zizek points out, choice is always a meta-choice, a choice of the modality and grounds of the choice itself:

> That is why, in our secular societies of choice, people who maintain a substantial religious belonging find themselves in a subordinate position; if they are allowed to practise their belief, this belief is 'tolerated' as their idiosyncratic personal choice; the moment they present it publicly as a matter of substantial belonging, they are accused of 'fundamentalism'. What this means is that the 'subject of free choice' (in the Western 'tolerant' multicultural sense) can

emerge only as the result of an extremely violent process of being torn out one's world, being cut off from one's roots.

(Zizek, 2006: 18)

Humanists are good at identifying the sacred values of others, and pointing out that they are relative, but bad at realising the same point applies to themselves. Their ethical relativism is subject to a selective blindness, according to which everyone's moral beliefs are relative except their own. Just like religious believers, many humanists react with moral outrage when someone dares even to *analyse* — let alone dispute — one or more of their sacred values. Tetlock describes moral outrage as a composite psychological state that subsumes cognitive reactions (such as attributing wicked motives to deviant thinkers), emotional responses (like anger and contempt), and actions (ostracising and punishing the deviant thinkers). Humanists often react to religion not like intuitive scientists seeking to understand causal relations, but as intuitive moralists/theologians struggling to protect sacred values from secular encroachments (Tetlock, 2003). They accuse religious believers of intolerance and criticise them for taking offence, yet display similar intolerance and take offence just as readily. Worse, they take offence at the idea that others take offence, betraying a peculiarly self-contradictory form of hypocrisy.

In other words, many humanists are guilty of a secular form of fundamentalism that is not very different from the religious fundamentalism they oppose. When two opposed fundamentalisms meet, we get something very like the clash of civilisations envisaged by Samuel Huntington (Huntington, 1996), though it would be more accurate to borrow Tariq Ali's expression, and talk about a 'clash of fundamentalisms' (Ali, 1993). This was what happened in the row over the cartoons. The row would not have escalated into violence if secular newspaper editors had not engaged in the tit-for-tat gesture of republishing the offending cartoons.

Conclusion

The rise of religious fundamentalism in the Middle East and in the USA has been accompanied by a growing mood of intolerance among humanists and secularists towards expressions of religious faith. This intolerance represents a kind of secular fundamentalism that is arguably even worse than the religious fundamentalism it opposes, because humanist fundamentalism is not even logically consistent. There is no ultimate authority—no divine lawgiver—to which humanists can appeal to sanction their moral principles, and so they must accept some form of moral relativism. So when they seek to impose their moral principles on others, or treat them as absolutes, they are not only being hypocrites; they are being inconsistent too.

As Frank Furedi has argued, secular fundamentalism is particularly evident in reactions to religious films. First there was the controversy provoked by Mel Gibson's *The Passion of the Christ* in 2004, and in 2005 *The Lion, The Witch and The Wardrobe* was bitterly condemned by liberal critics for its religious content. Furedi wrote:

> Such fervour reminds me of the way that reactionaries in the past policed Hollywood for hints of blasphemy or expressions of 'Un-American values'. Replacing the zealotry of religious intolerance with a secular version is hardly an enlightened alternative (Furedi, 2006).

But Furedi himself seems to fall prey to the same lack of imagination that underlies secular fundamentalism when he writes that 'in Gibson's vision Jesus is reduced to little more than a lump of meat, the victim of whippings and abuse whose physical suffering is shown in gruesome detail. It is far from uplifting.' Such a description betrays the purely secular viewpoint from which Furedi is writing. I too reacted in a similar way when I first saw the film. Indeed, I had to stop the DVD at the point where Jesus was being whipped, as I could not bear to see such bloody violence. It seemed so gratuitous, and it felt wrong to watch a man being tortured.

But then I realised that, to a Christian viewer, this was not simply 'a man being tortured'. To a Christian, this was the

Son of God, suffering to redeem our sins. And I recalled what that great humanist, David Hume, had to say about appreciating works of art:

> We may observe, that every work of art, in order to pro-
> duce its due effect on the mind, must be surveyed in a cer-
> tain point of view, and not be fully relished by persons,
> whose situation, real or imaginary, is not conformable to
> that which is required by the performance (Hume, 1757).

In viewing Gibson's film from my own, secular viewpoint, I had been like the man who, in Hume's words, 'obstinately maintains his natural position, without placing himself in that point of view, which the performance supposes.' Hume condemns this lack of imagination in no uncertain terms:

> If the work be addressed to persons of a different age or
> nation, he makes no allowance for their peculiar views and
> prejudices; but, full of the manners of his own age and
> country, rashly condemns what seemed admirable in the
> eyes of those for whom alone the discourse was calculated.
> [...] By this means, his sentiments are perverted; nor have
> the same beauties and blemishes the same influence upon
> him, as if he had imposed a proper violence on his imagina-
> tion, and had forgotten himself for a moment. So far his
> taste evidently departs from the true standard; and of con-
> sequence loses all credit and authority (Hume, 1757).

Hume is particularly keen to point out the relevance of such a principle to religious art:

> On this account, all the absurdities of the pagan system of
> theology must be overlooked by every critic, who would
> pretend to form a just notion of ancient poetry; and our pos-
> terity, in their turn, must have the same indulgence to their
> forefathers. No religious principles can ever be imputed as
> a fault to any poet (Hume, 1757).

So, taking Hume at his word, I proceeded to watch *The Passion of the Christ* again, from the beginning, and to 'impose a proper violence on my imagination' while doing so. I endeavoured, that is, to see it from a Christian point of view. It was quite hard at first. But as I grew accustomed to this alien perspective, the film began to affect me in a completely different way. With my Christian hat on, so to speak, I no longer saw a pointless act of torture, but a beautiful act of redemption. And instead of feeling repelled by the brutality, I was moved to tears by this act of divine love.

The experience did not turn me into a Christian. When the film ended (for I saw it through to the end this time) I took off my Christian hat, and put my atheist one back on. But I had gained something in that temporary holiday from my own belief-system. I had become aware of how different things seem from a religious point of view. I wish more of my fellow humanists would try to do the same.

References

Ali, T, 1993, *The Clash of Fundamentalisms: Crusades, Jihads and Modernity*, London: Verso.

Evans, D, 2005, 'The 21st century atheist', *The Guardian*, 2 May 2005.

Furedi, F. 2006, 'The curious rise of anti-religious hysteria' *spiked*, 23 January
http://www.spiked-online.com/articles/0000000CAF37.htm

Grayling, Anthony C, 2004, 'A wish for 2005', BBC News Online, http://news.bbc.co.uk/1/hi/world/4117901.stm

Hume, D, 1757, 'Of the standard of taste'

Huntington, SP, 1996, *The Clash of Civilizations and the Remaking of World Order*, New York: Simon & Schuster.

Rawls, J, 1995, *Political Liberalism*, New York: Columbia University Press.

Rushdie, S, 2005, 'Just give me that old-time atheism!', *Toronto Star*, 23 May

Tetlock, PE, Kristel, O, Elson, B, Green, M, and Lerner, J, 2000, 'The psychology of the unthinkable: Taboo trade-offs, forbidden base rates, and heretical counterfactuals', *Journal of Personality and Social Psychology*, 78, 853-870

Zizek, S, 2006, 'Our cherished friend Liberty reveals herself as a naked lie', *The Times Higher Educational Supplement*, 24 March

Frank Furedi

The Legacy of Humanism

It is easy to dismiss the legacy of humanism. All too often humanism presents itself in a caricatured form. Often it seems that it can only come alive through reliving its past struggles with religious dogma. Thus most people regard humanism as a secular movement defined by its hostility to religion and its passionate affirmation of atheism. This view is not surprising since many humanists take pride in their secular values and attach great importance to their anti-religious sentiments. This standpoint is clearly expressed in *A Humanist Manifesto* written in 1933 and signed by many prominent humanists. Although this manifesto traces the foundation of humanism to the exercise of reason, its main focus is to settle scores with religion. There is little doubt that humanism emerged through a conflict with organised religion. But it is much more than that. It is not a secular cult of man but an open-ended perspective that seeks to grasp the truth through human experience. As Sartre argued, humanism is not a static project but an orientation realised through the exercise of human subjectivity (Sartre, 1989).

Throughout history many progressive thinkers could not resist the temptation of trying to turn humanism into a dogma. Yet one of the most attractive and important dimension of humanistic thinking was its rejection of the need for a fixed system of ideas. Humanists did not simply reject religion because they had a superior secular faith but because they recognised that the search for the truth required an open-ended orientation to experience. Truth does not exist in stable and fixed form. Its attainment demands a constant commitment to exploration. Nor are there general truths waiting to be revealed. There are truths but they are truths only for a specific moment in time. The relative character of truth, however does not mean that humanism is based on a relativistic epistemology. It does not renounce objectivity; rather it specifies objectivity in relation to the problem it confronts.

Atheism does not constitute a world view. It simply expresses a rejection of God. It reflects an attitude towards one specific issue and not a perspective on the world. Humanism does not merely reject a belief in God but in dogma in all of its forms — secular and religious. The importance of humanism does not lie in what it rejects but in what it upholds. It upholds the importance of human experience as the foundation for knowledge. The understanding that emerges through this experience has provided people with the capacity to change their circumstances and through that process to transform their humanity. It is through the interaction between human thought and social experience that society becomes humanised and learns to move forward. Humanism does not provide answers about future directions, it merely facilitates the process whereby subjectivity can be exercised and develop through learning from new experience. Humanists are continually forced to rework their ideas in line with the new problems and insights thrown up by history. This can be a very exhausting challenge even for the best of us. Often it can distract us from grasping the issues that confront us.

Those who identify with humanism today are deeply concerned with the influence of Creationism and of movements variously described as fundamentalist Christian or the religious right. Anxieties about the apparent impact of these movements and the values they espouse inform the deliberations of humanist circles. Yet while attempts to reverse the separation of church and state are always a cause for concern, the real challenge facing humanists does not emanate from organised religion. Probably the most important challenge facing humanism is the growing cultural valuation of misanthropy. There is a powerful mood of disenchantment with humanity and its potential for playing a positive and creative role. And the sources for these influences are more often than not secular rather than religious.

Many influential theories — Intelligent design, Gaia theory, Chaos theory — self consciously render the human subject marginal. But often critics of religious obscurantism like Creationism are oblivious to a more influential tendency to regard human beings as just another species. The influence of *environmental determinism* is particularly striking. From this standpoint human beings are assigned a minor and undistinguished role in the general scheme of things. And any attempt by people to gain control over their destiny is likely to be undermined by the forces of nature. Moreover the very attempt to control nature is represented as an act of a destructive species which does not know its place in the natural order of things. Instead of celebrating man's attempt to transform nature, commentators recast history and civilisation as a story of environmental destruction. From this standpoint the application of reason, knowledge and science are dismissed as problems because they help intensify the destructive capacity of the human species. 'Humans are, literally, a species out of control', notes a misanthropic contribution (Cairns, 2005: 1). From this perspective humanism itself is the problem.

Indeed there is a widespread conviction that it is the development of human civilisation, particularly the advance of science and technology, and the resulting subordination of the natural order to the demands of human society, that is the source of today's problems of environmental destruction and social disintegration. The perception that it is civilisation that bears responsibility for the perils we face today assigns an undistinguished if not low status to the human species. At times this sentiment expresses a sense of loathing for the human species. Such sentiments are expressed by Earth First when they chant 'Four Legs Good! Two Legs Bad!' Indeed people are regularly portrayed as loathsome parasites who threaten the existence of the earth.

As I have written elsewhere the real challenge facing humanism is the low esteem accorded to the status of humanity (Furedi, 2005). The world today is dominated by a widespread disenchantment with the record of humanity's achievement. There is a manifest lack of confidence in the capacity of people to reason and influence the course of events. The past is frequently represented as a sordid tale of people destroying the planet. The construction of a past that continually highlights human selfishness and destruction helps the current project of dispossessing people of any unique or positive qualities.

The depiction of human activity as itself a threat to the world tends to endow this species with an overwhelmingly negative status. Instead of positive transformation and progress, civilisation is portrayed as a history of environmental vandalism. This misanthropic sentiment was clearly expressed by Michael Meacher, the former Labour Minister for the Environment when in 2003, he spoke about how 'we are the virus' infecting the Earth's body. His colleague, Labour MP Tony Banks echoed expressed a similar sentiment in his proposed motion to the House of Commons. It stated that 'This House.. believes that humans represent the most obscene, perverted, cruel, uncivilised and lethal speciess ever to inhabit the planet and looks forward to the day when the inevitable asteroid slams into the Earth and wipes them out thus giving Nature the opportunity to start again' (Banks, 2004). Of course such intense loathing for people represents but an extreme variant of contemporary anti-humanism.

The prevailing climate of misanthropy is the product of disillusionment with the consequences of change. The intense scepticism regarding the desirability of change is strongly reflected in a powerful sense of estrangement from a fundamental idea associated with humanism—that of progress. There is no perceptible difference in political attitude towards the question of progress: the nineteenth century model of left-wing enthusiasm and right-wing suspicion no longer has relevance. In the 21st century it is difficult to find any systematic intellectual defence of the idea of progress. On the contrary, the idea of progress is usually indicted for encouraging human arrogance and destructiveness. The attempt to exercise control over our destiny is frequently dismissed as an exercise in Promethean arrogance. Those who search for new solutions and engage in experimentation are castigated for 'playing God'. Others seek to restrain scientific investigation in case it opens up a Pandora's Box. Implicitly the condemnation of the idea of progress contains a warning against the aspiration for making or changing history. Rejecting the ideal of progress means demanding that we accept our Fate.

The current reaction against the idea of progress is one of the most unfortunate consequences of the decline of influence of Enlightenment thinking. Its consequence is to encourage deference to Fate and disengagement from taking responsibility for controlling our future. According to this model change acquires an objectified form so that we have history without a subject. This suppression of the historical subject has important implication of the way we regard people. The downsizing of the role of the subject has as its premise the rejection of the humanist ideal of personhood.

The prevailing sense of diminished subjectivity is underwritten by a distinct code about the workings of human behaviour and personhood. Every culture provides a set of ideas and beliefs about the nature of human beings and what constitutes their personhood. Our ideas about what we can expect from one another, how we handle uncertainty and change, deal with adversity and pain and how we view history are underpinned by the particular account that a culture offers about personhood and the human potential. The defining feature of the current Western 21st century version of personhood is its *vulnerability*. Although society still upholds the ideals of self-determination and autonomy the values associated with them are increasingly overridden by a more dominant message that stresses the quality of human weakness. The model of human vulnerability and powerlessness is transmitted through powerful ideas that call into question people's capacity to assume a measure of control over their affairs. Social commentators regularly declare that we live in the era of the 'death of the subject', 'the death of the author', 'decentred subject', 'end of history' or 'end of politics'. Such pessimistic accounts of the human potential inform both intellectual and cultural life in the west. They provide cultural legitimation for the downsizing human ambition.

Humanising humanism

It is perverse that 21st society, which relies so much on human ingenuity and science also encourages deference to Fate. At a time of widespread disenchantment with the record of humanity's achievements, it important to restore confidence in the capacity of people to reason and influence the course of events. This is a challenge that confronts everyone who upholds a human centred orientation towards the world. This task may appear as a modest one compared to the grand visions of the past but in our anti-humanist pre-political era its realisation is a precondition for the restoration of a climate hospitable to politics.

The reconstitution of the sense of agency and of historical thinking is the prerequisite for the reengagement of the public with political life. That requires that we uphold humanity's past achievements, including standards of excellence and civilised forms of behaviour and values. Far from representing a yearning for the good old days, over-coming our alienation from the legacy of human achieve-ment helps us deal with the issues thrown by change. It is through drawing on the achievements of the past that we can embrace change with enthusiasm.

Promoting a consistent belief in human potential under-pins progressive thought. A human-centred view of the world recognises that people can be destructive and that conflicts of interests can lead to devastating outcomes. However, the negative and sometimes horrific experiences of the past two centuries, up to and including the Holocaust, are not the price of progress, but of the lack of it. Contempo-rary problems are not the result of applying reason, science and knowledge, but of neglecting them and thwarting the human potential.

The humanist intellectual universe needs to be ambitious but open-ended, prepared to countenance the validity of any idea and ready to yield to new experience. Such a perspective must engage in the process of *humanising humanism*. Humanising humanism requires that failure and mistakes are incorporated into the way we regard progress and the exercise of rationality. If human agency is assigned an important role in the making of history than factors like culture, subjective perception, conflict, contingency and limited knowledge all play a role in the way we engage with the world. Such influences can confuse, distract and disorient. Nevertheless they provide some of the important experiences from which we learn how to move forward. In a sense progress happens through these experiences in the exercise of subjectivity. Humanising humanism requires that we stop treating human development as a foregone conclusion. What we need is a humanism that is not a dogma but a perspective oriented to learning from what humans do.

When the inclination is to wallow in the dark side of humanity, it is worth emphasising that the legacy of the Enlightenment has provided us with a high standard of moral and ethical responsibility. The twentieth century has witnessed appalling atrocities and relapses into barbarism and genocide. Yet though the scale of degradation experienced in modern society may have been greater than in earlier times, it is only in our era that such events would have been popularly regarded with moral opprobrium. Torture, slavery, the slaughter of defeated enemies — before the modern era such activities were generally considered legitimate and went without question. Autocracy, hierarchy, elitism were considered to be features of a natural order vested with divine authority. It is only with the emergence of modern society, with its concepts of democracy and equality that the possibility of progress and of the improvement of humanity in both material and moral sense arises.

It is ironic that sentiments of moral revulsion against the evils of modern society are often accompanied by a tendency to repudiate the framework of rationality and purposeful intervention in nature and society that make a more truly human society possible. What we need is a more balanced assessment of the state of society, one that rejects the gross exaggeration of problems and recognises what we have achieved. But most important of all we need to understand that whatever the mistakes that we have made we can extract from them lessons that can guide us to move forward. The reconstitution of agency does not require the invention of grand philosophies but the humanising of humanism through empowering personhood.

References

Banks, Tony, 2004, Early Day Motion 1255, 21 May, Parliamentary Information Management Services

Cairns, J, 2005 'Transitions: Speculative Futures For Homo Sapiens', *Science and Society*, vol.3, no.2, 2005

Furedi, Frank, 2005, *The Politics of Fear: Beyond Left and Right*, Continuum Press.

The New Humanist, 1933 'A Humanist Manifesto' May/June

Sartre, Jean-Paul 'Existentialism Is A Humanism' (lecture given in 1946), republished in Kaufman, W (ed), 1989, *Existentialism from Dostoyevski to Sartre*, Meridian Publishing Company

Elisabeth Lasch-Quinn

Morality and the Crisis of Secularisation

Few would deny that politics and culture in the West face alarming problems, though not everyone would trace those problems to a crisis in secularism. Many of those who hold a secularist perspective, in particular, still take the position: what crisis? If they accept the diagnosis of a crisis, which they often do not, they point instead to the tenacity of out-moded beliefs and superstitions. The culprit for them is religion. If only religionists could give up their irrational, fatalistic worldview and get with the programme of modernity, our problems could be solved so much more easily. Science is the knight in shining armour and technology the glorious white steed to save the day.

In turn, many religious believers — thinking of themselves as dyed in the wool when they may actually have acquired their beliefs yesterday in a born-again-moment in one of US's mega churches or sitting on their sofas viewing a televised ministry — often view nonbelievers as the main problem. That the tragedy of 9/11 is our comeuppance for our religious delinquency is only the most callous and extreme notion put forth by this camp. If only the heathen would convert, God would smile on us.

Fundamentalist secularism and fundamentalist religion sadly hold great sway today. Both benefit today from the power of the pulpit, as the modern communications media parasitically home in on the most extreme positions and drastic oppositions in pursuit of the audience's attention (translation: ratings and money). Ferreting out the most dichotomous positions stands in for investigative reporting and political engagement and edges out wiser voices among the secularists and religionists vital for any significant and meaningful political debate. Voices that come from the substantial depths that exist in between narrowly secularist and religious positions — depths from which any sense of commonality, however limited, might emerge — remain unheard and unheeded. Yet these depths are our only remaining hope.

In his 1991 book, *Why Americans Hate Politics*, journalist E J Dionne pointed out that one of the reasons for the low rates of political engagement in the US was that the stands on key issues such as abortion taken by the two political parties did not represent what many so-called ordinary citizens thought when they considered the issues. In particular, polarised debates such as that over abortion did not seem to people to capture the moral complexities involved. In the decade and a half since Dionne's book, the political positions on hot-button issues have, if anything, become even more rigid, with little possibility of other options. Briefly, President Clinton seemed to offer an alternative, through his notion of the 'New Democrat,' combining some of the moral vigour and fiscal responsibility then associated with the right with the commitment to social justice of the left. And 'Compassionate Conservatism' promised to humanise a political right that often seemed military-obsessed and ruthless in its approach to the poor and others excluded from the American dream of prosperity and justice. Both fell far short of delivering on their promises. Neither has proven a significant alternation or presented fresh views on divisive issues, let alone represented the complexities of the daunting issues we face.

One such complexity, of course, is that over the course of the last couple of centuries, there surfaced a significant questioning of religious belief and a reorganisation of life along secular lines. Whether one views this change as progress or tragedy, it represents a major shift in how individuals make sense of the world around them. True, many still possess a profound faith, but it is just as true that many do not. And for many of today's believers, the substance of their belief and the role it plays in their lives take a back seat to their secular concerns. In his *Triumph of the Therapeutic: Uses of Faith after Freud*, published in 1966, Philip Rieff charted the transition from a predominantly religious to a purely therapeutic worldview. He also began to articulate a theory of culture, which held that a common commitment to the sacred — a sense of transcendent purpose — lies at the heart of any viable culture. What a culture gives the individual is a 'saving self' that is larger that the individual's self. It does this by passing down traditions, ideals, beliefs, and the institutions that embody them, in the form of morality, the distinction between what should and should not be done. Culture thus releases individuals from the tyranny of their own needs and impulses — and the psychic isolation to which we are prone — precisely through its 'permissions' and 'restraints,' which take the seemingly unlimited desires we experience and channels them into 'fixed wants' that can be fulfilled. Without a common sense that there is something sacred, life in society becomes nothing more than instrumentalist manipulation of everybody else for one's own purposes. Individual gratification becomes the new creed, but the absence of the means of any kind of profound gratification makes the search for gratification never-ending.

The therapeutic culture enshrines a certain notion of the individual, one that casts humans as enslaved to their desires and inherently possessed with the right to boundless personal freedom. This ethos has emerged hand-in-hand with the rise of consumerism as a way of life, including its most recent variant, niche marketing, which no longer presupposes certain common wants underlying the mass marketing of the 1950s and 1960s but instead places the idiosyncratic desires of customers, however shallow or perverse, on a pedestal. Market demand trumps all other imperatives.

Political theorist Mary Ann Glendon eloquently warned of the dangers of hyper-individualism in her 1991 book *Rights Talk: The Impoverishment of Political Discourse*. Exaggerated claims of personal entitlements and freedoms threatened to erode the body politic itself by attacking the civic bonds and sense of responsibility on which these things relied. An overly 'strident' defence of rights, she argued, actually took away the basis on which rights and liberty rest, by contributing 'to the erosion of the habits, practices, and attitudes of respect for others that are the ultimate and surest guarantors of human rights.' Glendon saw these practices and views as renewed by alternative social traditions still extant by the time she wrote in 1991 but which the dominant political culture threatened to render obsolete. These entailed 'cooperative, relational, patterns of living,' such as those still promulgated by many women, who 'nourished a sense of connectedness between individuals, and an awareness of the linkage among present, past, and future generations' or the 'Biblical language of stewardship' of some conservationists, who came to realise the limits of such appeals as 'endowing trees with rights.'

The modern cult of the individual and its needs apart from its community membership or its cultural context has dovetailed with the moral relativism that traditional religious culture left in its wake. Philosopher Alasdair MacIntyre recounted the rise of 'emotivism,' by which claims one might make in argument can be subjected to no court of appeal, in the absence of a common standard of truth, other than the subjective beliefs of the isolated individual. He describes a modern culture in disarray, devoid of a coherent moral framework.

This essay aims merely to raise the question — and perhaps cling to the quaint hope — of an alternative to such a vicious dichotomy between religious and secular views. For one of the most promising ways to address the crisis in secularism — but one that is rarely attempted — would be to refuse to fall prey to the simplistic dichotomy between secular and religious visions of humanity. A creative fusion of religious and secular humanism that searches for points of commonality and affinity, common intellectual sources and traditions, and shared moral premises but at the same time acknowledges the inherent tensions between competing visions is not just desirable but perhaps also necessary, if any form of humanism is to survive, given today's culture wars.

Even if we do not agree with the secularists' diagnosis that to yearn for some things that we have lost is to go backwards, we cannot go back entirely whence we came as if history did not happen. And it is taking the benefits science has brought us for granted to long for religion to replace science, in the fundamentalists' terms, as though science never existed. But neither can secularists claim to be the party of the future, with so shrunken a moral vision. Both rabid secularism, which denies all claims of religion and its continuing service as a foundation for morality for so many, and fundamentalist religion have the faults of a purging utopianism, wishing for a wholesale reorganisation of life so as to legislate permanently a state of bliss, free from the complicated entanglements and tensions of everyday life.

There is much richer ground that remains to be tilled. What about the scientists who were religious believers? Might the study of their views help us think differently about issues that threaten to pit us against ourselves, such as human cloning? What about theologians who understood the great fruits and truths of science? Might we articulate a new notion of the sacred that appeals to some limited degree to religionists and secularists alike? Could we at least restore some kind of moral consensus, even if we do not allow that it has divine sanction? What about commonalities between the more compelling manifestations of religious and secular traditions, such as the belief in the dignity of the human person and in stewardship? Could that not be starting point for a more widely shared sense of the underpinnings of morality? A reconsideration of the meaning and ideal of democracy — a commitment still shared by most religionists and secularists in the West today — is another possible starting point for a reinvigoration of humanism today. Alexis de Tocqueville, whose great work *Democracy in America* captured with such intricacy and eloquence the hopes and dreams of the new republic just a generation after its founding, defined democracy as 'a habit of the heart.' Despite their important differences, the founders' shared spirit and common moral understanding breathed life into the laws, governmental structures, and social forms of the new nation, thus affecting the social, cultural, political, and intellectual experience of Americans down to the current day. Including but not reducible to a particular political system or set of social arrangements — from enfranchisement and representative government to rights, freedom, and justice — the notion of a democratic republic involved a sensibility, a disposition, or, one might say, a pre-disposition.

Concerns arise daily from across the political spectrum about whether Americans remain pre-disposed to democracy. Observers point to a widening gap between rich and poor unheard of since the Gilded Age, corporate dominance of political campaigns and the airwaves, low levels of voting and civic engagement, an ethos of extreme individualism that values self-gratification over commitments to others, corruption in government and business, the decline of the family and civil society institutions, the crisis of morality and civility, and many other symptoms of a society at the breaking point. What is more, while once reformers might have interpreted these problems as cause for a renewal of ideals and effort, many contemporaries raise more fundamental questions about the ideals themselves. Are we witnessing the fall from greatness of Western democracies? The perception of political exhaustion is palpable. Some conservatives raise doubts about democracy itself and even on the political left, traditionally the party of the common person, a sense of despair is apparent in the grumblings about whether an elite might be necessary after all, given today's political situation.

Of the many problems faced by today's leading democratic nations, the loss of hope, confidence, and will may be its greatest threat. It is worth remembering Benjamin Franklin's caustic reply to the question of what kind of government we were to have: 'A republic, if you can keep it.' Together with their revolutionary ideals, the framers of the constitution expressed many reservations, worries, and doubts. Their enthusiasm was tempered by humility and awareness of human limitations. In their notion of republicanism, self-government entailed active participation, virtue, and vigilance against corruption and tyranny. Franklin went so far as to warn that the tendency is that 'the People shall become so corrupted as to need Despotic Government, being incapable of any other.'

The effort to keep our republic(s) has to include tapping deeply into the intellectual and political tradition, which many self-designated progressives were all too happy to leave behind as a relic of the benighted past. This vital interlacing of tradition and dissent characterises both the prodigious contribution of the founding generation and the tradition of the public intellectual, which has included more recent writers such as John Dewey, Walter Lippman, Lionel Trilling, Reinhold Niebuhr, Alfred Kazin, Ralph Ellison, Daniel Patrick Moynihan, and Hannah Arendt, to name just a few. Several late-twentieth-century trends, including the tendency of many academic scholars to address just one small professional subfield, worked against this tradition, but there are many signs of a resurgence of interest in the vital connection between scholarship and broader public questions. Hannah Arendt wrote that 'the perplexity of laws in free societies is that they only tell what one should not, but never what one should do.' Only by keeping alive the tradition of free and open inquiry and deep learning, the ideal of the liberal arts education, can we call on the cultural tradition as a resource to help us discuss, debate, and deliberate over the multitude of issues that we face. The larger question—how we live together, broadly speaking—is the question of the public philosophy. In *Democracy's Discontent: America in Search of a Public Philosophy*, Michael Sandel has written, 'By public philosophy, I mean the political theory implicit in our practice, the assumptions about citizenship and freedom that inform our public life.' Sandel and others worry that the loss of a sense of our underlying commonalities makes disagreement threatening rather than fruitful. Mary Ann Glendon, Amitai Etzioni, and Jean Bethke Elshtain, among others, have made a compelling appeal for moving beyond a rights-based ethos that emphasises our differences and entitlements to one based on a sense of common commitments and shared principles.

Public intellectual work and those dedicated to the liberal arts have the potential to play an invaluable part in renewing the discussion of the public philosophy under secularism, resuscitating democratic politics and public discourse, and in retrieving — and newly formulating — the ethical foundations of our common life. It is a particularly auspicious time for a deepening understanding of both secular and religious humanism and for adding to our sense of their common ground. The time is ripe for those who seek a renewal of the republican principles and a revitalisation of democratic politics toward a sense of common purpose and dedication to the decent and open society and the common good.

Answering the questions posed by the crisis of secularism is beyond the scope of this brief essay — and perhaps will prove to be beyond the scope of mankind itself. In all of the best thinking on the subject there surfaces a nagging question. What if the most virulent secularists and religionists have actually stumbled on a kind of truth: what if religion and secularism really are, quite simply, incompatible? In the words of the bard Bob Dylan, 'You either have faith or you have unbelief / There ain't no neutral ground.'

The only way to answer this, given the particular historical moment in which we live, is to hope — or to pray, depending on one's proclivities — that this is somehow not the case.

References

De Tocqueville, Alexis, 2000 (1835, 1840) *Democracy in America*, ed Harvey Mansfield; trans. Delba Winthrop, Chicago: University of Chicago Press, 2000.

Dionne, EJ, 1991, *Why Americans Hate Politics*, NY: Simon and Schuster

Glendon, Mary Ann, 1991, *Rights Talk: The Impoverishment of Political Discourse* New York: The Free Press

MacIntyre, Alasdair, 1981, *After Virtue: A Study in Moral Theory*, Notre Dame: University of Notre Dame Press

Rieff, Philip, 1987 (1966), *The Triumph of the Therapeutic: Uses of Faith after Freud*, Chicago: University of Chicago Press

Sandel, Michael J, 1996, *Democracy's Discontent: America in Search of a Public Philosophy* Cambridge, MA: Belknap Press of Harvard University Press

Vidal, Gore, 2003, *Inventing a Nation: Washington, Adams, Jefferson*, New Haven, CT: Yale University Press

Anthony Freeman

Christian Humanism

I

From the dawn of civilisation religion had stood centre-stage in public life. Then, a mere 300 years ago, the Enlightenment and the Age of Reason changed the whole character and role of organised religion. Outward forms might still be observed — the quasi-priestly British monarch is still anointed in the manner of King Solomon (accompanied by Handel's *Zadok* to ram the point home) — but the power had drained away. Public worship declined into an optional past-time; religion became privatised to the extent that AN Whitehead could declare 'Religion is what the individual does with his own solitariness … if you are never solitary, you are never religious' (Whitehead, 1926).

Now the old religion is fighting back. It is reasserting its traditional role in public and political life. Especially in the US, but increasingly in Britain as well, conservative religious forces are combining to challenge and direct domestic policy in areas like education (teaching creationism), medical research (stem cells), personal relations (same-sex partnerships) and clinical treatment (abortion, euthanasia). Nor is the fighting metaphorical only. A heady mix of religion, politics and nationalism leads daily to the violent clashes between Sikh and Hindu, Catholic and Protestant, Muslim and Jew, them and us, my lot and your lot.

All this action has provoked its own reaction. So long as modern religion stayed quiet, limited to a ceremonial backdrop in public and individual piety in private, it could live at peace with its increasingly powerful successor, the scientific and humanistic world view. Academics might debate the clash between science and religion, but everyone else could enjoy the fruits of technology alongside their chosen faith or superstition with no apparent sense of conflict. Now such easy-going live-and-let live days are over. The time has come to call traditional religion to account, and high profile figures from science and philosophy — such as Richard Dawkins and Daniel Dennett — are being given ample space to do it by mainstream broadcasters and publishers.

External criticism, however, tends merely to polarise the argument, and has no logical ending except the complete destruction of either the religious or the secular position. Much as extremists on either side might relish such an outcome, a less drastic solution to the ill effects of religion, namely the internal reform of inappropriate religious claims and aspirations, is more likely to succeed. Dennett himself, in more conciliatory moments, has called for a combined effort by moderate religious leaders and secularists to put an end to extremist religion. I can hardly claim these days to be a religious leader, having been dismissed from my parish in 1994 and subsequently refused permission by a string of bishops to exercise a public ministry. Nor, perhaps, does the term 'moderate' any longer fit me, since the cause of this episcopal abhorrence is my rejection of the supernatural concept of God, and by most reckoning that is a pretty extreme position for a priest to hold. But with little sign of the Church's official leaders responding to Dennett's call, they will have to be satisfied with me.

II

I use the term Christian Humanism to denote a particular way of interpreting the Christian tradition, which acknowledges that being human is more fundamental than belonging to any particular religious or racial grouping (Freeman, 2001). It is a term that irritates secular humanists and traditionalist Christians in equal measure, both sides objecting that Christianity has God at its centre, while humanism — as the term is used today — has no place for God at all. This objection misses the essential point that a human being,

Jesus Christ, is at the centre of Christianity. Moreover, there is a strand of teaching going back to the New Testament itself that nothing can be known of God except that which is known through Christ, in his human life. (John 1: 'No one has ever seen God. It is God the only Son [ie Jesus Christ], who is close to the Father's heart, who has made him known'.) This means that Christianity does not start off with the term 'god' as popularly understood by scientists, philosophers and other religions. In particular, it does not arbitrarily define God as a supernatural agent, separate from and prior to the created order, including the human race. Christians should claim no knowledge about God other than what they necessarily learn of God through Jesus Christ, and that does not include anything supernatural. On the contrary, when it remains true to its origins in the human Jesus, Christianity is able to offer today's world a religious alternative both to superstition and to secularism.

The seeds of this humanistic approach to knowledge of God may be found in the belief, inherited from Judaism, that humankind was made in God's image, an image that the early Christians believed had been renewed and perfected in the person of Jesus Christ. I am sure that the writers of the New Testament did believe in God as a supernatural and eternal being. Even so, the pattern of theology that they laid down, with Christ at the centre, prepares us, indeed it requires us, to abandon earlier misconceptions and develop an understanding of God that is 'Christ shaped' and therefore 'human shaped'.

We also find in Christianity's Jewish heritage a strong prophetic tradition, from which there emerges a portrait of Israel's God that looks more like an anti-god, one who contradicts everything that the ancient world expected of its deities. First he refused to give his name. Every god needed a name by which his devotees could call upon him, but when God first appeared to Moses in the burning bush, setting in train the Exodus from Egypt, he absolutely refused to give his name. Moses begged him, but God was adamant: I AM THAT I AM. Tell them I AM has sent you (Exodus 3). He would not reveal his name, or even admit to having one.

The next thing every god needed was some physical token of his presence, an image to focus the people's attention. But again, not the God of Israel: Thou shalt not make unto thyself any graven image (Exodus 20). Nor did he allow a temple in his honour, at least not for hundreds of years after Moses' time. So how were you meant to worship him? Well, it seems he did not want to be worshipped either. As the prophet Amos said in his name: 'I hate, I despise your feasts, and I take no delight in your solemn assemblies. Take away from me the noise of your songs.' And Hosea: 'I desire mercy, not sacrifice; and knowledge of God more than burnt offerings.'

No name, no image, no temple, no worship ... it all adds up to no god — at least no god in the accepted sense of the word. And this is the Bible's own account of its own God! Or rather, one of its accounts. The Old Testament can be read as a battle between two views of God. On one side was the religion of the priesthood and the temple, which said Israel's God was basically just like other gods, it was just that he was the best. On the other side were the prophets, for whom the belief that there was only one God *for Israel* developed into the belief that there was *only one God*. Full stop. This was monotheism and it was the great prophets who were not only persuaded of its truth, but also grasped how great an inherent danger it carried.

When you had a lot of competing gods of the traditional kind, they acted as a set of checks and balances against each other; but a single such god would be unchallenged and all-powerful — a cosmic dictator — an appalling prospect. This is the intuition behind the insistence of the Old Testament prophets that the God of Israel — if he were indeed the only God — must be radically unlike any previous concept of a god. The subsequent war-torn history of the three monotheistic religions fully justifies their fears; their willingness *in the name of God* to overturn all currently accepted notions of deity provides a model and an inspiration today for all religious — especially Christian — humanists.

III

To see what a contemporary humanist doctrine of God-made-known-in-Christ might look like, we need to look at how ideas about the human person have changed since the classic Christian formulae were hammered out in the fifth century. The early Church was dominated by Neoplatonic philosophy. With minor variations, a human was thought of as a fusion of two separate parts, a non-material soul or mind and a physical body. These came together at conception or birth and were separated at death. In the seventeenth and eighteenth centuries, when many other religious ideas came under fire from the scholars of the Enlightenment, mind/body dualism received a boost from the widely accepted distinction made by Descartes between *res extensa*, which was physical, measurable, and locatable in space, and *res cogitans*, which was none of these things. Today the situation is quite different. Among philosophers of mind, psychologists and neurophysiologists, Descartes is normally mentioned only to be scorned or refuted, and 'dualist' is almost a term of abuse.

So if our conscious mind (or soul) is not a separate entity that comes from outside to be associated with our body, what is it? And where does it come from? The most general answer, on which most scholars would agree, is that it comes from our physical body. Beyond that, opinions differ. Some say that our state of mind at any particular moment simply *is* the state of our brain, without remainder. The conscious mind is not something extra to or different from the brain — there is no ghost in the machine — rather the mind is simply the brain 'seen from the inside' as it were.

In its most extreme version, this physicalist view eliminates the reality of the mind altogether. It holds that subjective mental states are illusory, and that the physical brain is all there really is. Daniel Dennett espouses this view, or something very close to it (Dennett, 1993). A more moderate account — known as the 'dual aspect' theory — goes back at least to Spinoza in the seventeenth century, and was championed also by the twentieth-century humanist and philosopher Bertrand Russell, who called it 'neutral monism'

(Russell, 1970). This holds that the material and the mental are two different aspects of some underlying and more fundamental reality.

Yet another interpretation — and this is the one of particular interest here — relies on the concept of 'emergence'. While maintaining that the mind is wholly physical in origin, arising in the brain and continuously associated with it, this approach nonetheless says that once having 'emerged', the mind does constitute something extra in the world. The 'whole' of the brain/mind is more than the sum of its physical parts. Emergence theory comes in various forms. Some emphasise the physicalist side — eg John Searle, with his formula that the mind is 'caused by' and 'realised in' the brain (Searle, 1984: 21) — while others are more radical and come close to old-fashioned dualism (Hasker, 1999).

IV

These contemporary approaches to the 'mind–body problem', as it is sometimes called, can bring a surpisingly fresh look to Christianity's ancient doctrinal formulations. One of these, the so-called 'Athanasian Creed' (fifth century), states that the human and the divine were related in Jesus Christ in precisely the same way as the physical body and the rational soul are related in all human beings:

> Perfect God, and Perfect Man: of a reasonable soul and human flesh subsisting; . . .
>
> Who although he be God and Man: yet he is not two, but one Christ; . . .
>
> For as the reasonable soul and flesh is one man: so God and Man is one Christ.
>
> (Translation from the *Book of Common Prayer*, 1662).

When a dualistic model of the human person was being used, this formula proclaimed an equally dualistic relation between God and man; but if the conscious mind is an emergent property of the physical brain, then the divine element in Christ is also to be understood as an emergent property. That is to say: just as Jesus' human mind — and indeed any human mind — arose from the complex physiology of his body, especially the brain and nervous system, so his divinity arose from his total humanity, body-and-mind.

On this view, just as the mind or soul is not an added ingredient to the human body, but an integral emergent property of it, so Christ's divinity is not an added ingredient to his human person, but an integral emergent property of it. Add to this my earlier statement — that Christians should claim no *a priori* knowledge of God, but only what they come to know through Christ — and the basic case for Christian Humanism is in place. On a non-dualistic Christ-centred account, God is not a supernatural agent external to humanity, but an emergent property of human life itself. This understanding of religion is faithful both to classic doctrinal formulae and to modern philosophy and science, and it has the potential to free Christians from supernaturalism and superstition without losing all that is still of positive value in their religion. In practical terms, it provides a platform within the Church to fight the aspects of resurgent fundamentalism whose destructive potential causes such anxiety to Dawkins, Dennett, and indeed all right-thinking people.

V

Lest this presentation of Christianity seem totally unorthodox, I should point out that some support for such an approach may be found among reputable theologians from the modern era. For instance, Friedrich Schleiermacher, a Protestant scholar known as the 'father of modern theology', wrote early in the nineteenth century that every human being has the capacity for what he called God-consciousness. He rejected the idea that Christ's divinity was something external to his humanity, insisting instead that it was 'the constant potency of his God-consciousness, which was a veritable existence of God in him'(Schleiermacher, 1989: 385). Christ, he wrote, is 'the one in Whom the creation of human nature ... was perfected' (Schleiermacher, 1989: 374). This language is very close to that of Karl Rahner, a leading twentieth-century

Catholic theologian, who wrote: 'Only someone who forgets that the essence of man is to be unbounded ... can suppose that it is impossible for there to be a man, who, *precisely by being man in the fullest sense* ... is God's existence in the world.' (Rahner, 1961: 184 — emphasis added) On this basis, you could almost say that Christianity is humanist by definition.

Schleiermacher was insistent that the divine aspect of Christ was not the result of any supernatural intervention but arose naturally with the perfecting of his humanity. It was not therefore unique to this one human person, but potentially open to all. Thus he also says, 'As certainly as Christ was a man, there must reside in human nature the possibility of taking up the divine into itself. ... So the idea that the divine revelation in Christ must be something in this respect supernatural will simply not stand the test' (Schleiermacher, 1989: 64). This way of interpreting the incarnation in terms of God-consciousness — that is as an emergent property — paves the way for the kind of Christian Humanism that I am developing. It is an authentic expression of both Christianity and Humanism at the beginning of the third millennium, and one that should enable secular and religious humanists to unite against the many inhumane forces — not least religious ones — that threaten the world today.

References

Dennett, Daniel, 1993, *Consciousness Explained*, Penguin

Freeman, Anthony, 2001, *God In Us: A Case for Christian Humanism* SCM Press, 1993; 2nd ed. Imprint Academic, 2001

Hasker, William, 1999, *The Emergent Self*, Cornell University Press

Schleiermacher, Friedrich, 1959, *The Christian Faith*, T & T Clark

Rahner, Karl, 1961, *Theological Investigations*, vol. 1, Darton, Longman & Todd

Russell, Bertrand, 1970, *An Outline of Philosophy*, Routledge

Searle, John 1984, *Minds, Brains and Science*, Harvard University Press

Whitehead, Alfred North, 1926, *Religion in the Making* (Lecture One) Harvard University

AC Grayling

Humanism, Religion, and Ethics

In its contemporary sense the term 'humanism' denotes the view that whatever ethical outlook we adopt, it has to be based on our best understanding of human nature and the human condition, and not on belief in the existence of supernatural agencies whose intentions or commands define moral reality and our place in it. Thus understood, humanism is expressly a secular, naturalistic outlook, sharply contrasted to religious systems of thought, whose fundamental premises it rejects.

The contemporary sense of the term 'humanism' descends from its origin as a label for the revival of classical learning in the period known as the Renaissance, because that learning focused on the surviving literary output of ancient Greece and Rome. That body of literature is the source for modern secular ethics because when in the seventeenth century it became possible to think afresh about the foundations of ethics, after more than a thousand years in which Christian doctrine dominated all ethical discourse and made foundational questions irrelevant, the thinkers of the early modern period turned to the classical sources for inspiration and guidance.

It matters that the outlook of classical antiquity should be properly understood for its humanistic spirit and tenour. This has been contested by some apologists for religion, on the ground that when some of the philosophers of antiquity made use of such notions as 'reason' and 'order' as metaphysical principles of organisation in the universe, they gave them, as a label of convenience, the name 'gods'. Religious apologists have wished to appropriate this manner of speaking in order to make it cognate to their own tradition. But unlike Judaism and the later religious movements of Christianity and Islam that arose from it, these personifying fictions were very remote from being conceived as personal creator deities so interested in their creatures that they took trouble to prescribe what could be eaten on what days, what clothing should be worn, who could have sexual relations with whom, and so (considerably) forth.

Indeed the differences between classical humanism and the religions that have become dominant after its time are great. The 'Religions of the Book' (Judaism, Christianity and Islam) are modelled on monarchy, the system in which authority resides in a paramount ruler to whom all must submit in hope of reward and for fear of punishment. Such a view would not only have been alien to the Greek classical mind, but repugnant to it. Where the religious concept of sin means disobedience to the punitive authority of an invisible dictator, the classical conception of wrongdoing was that of a misfire, as when an arrow flies wide of the mark; when in the course of his moral life an agent reflects upon his misfires, his purpose is the achievement of better aim next time.

Antiquity's humanistic spirit has been repeatedly asserted against the religious traditions which have enjoyed so large a dominance in the last two millennia. Some of the most brilliant moments of that assertion are given their own labels of convenience: the Renaissance, denoting the period between the fourteenth and seventeenth centuries in Europe, and its progeny the Enlightenment, which began in the eighteenth century and which stills wages war against the counter-Enlightenment forces of religion and totalitarianism, two forms of the same drive towards suppression of the central humanistic value of human autonomy.

Those who embrace the humanist outlook as meant here agree in nominating individual liberty, the pursuit of knowledge, the promotion of culture, and the fellowship of man, as guiding generalities when thinking about the good for humankind. Of course these are idealisations, and the hard grain of human experience shows how difficult it is to realise them in fact and in detail. It is the striving for their realisation that imparts nobility to human experience at its best and most hopeful, all the more so because human nature itself is too often in unconscious conspiracy with the conscious forces of anti-humanism to thwart them—these traitors in human nature being its tendencies to cupidity, stupidity, ignorance, laziness and cruelty.

The religious view—the view that says there are supernatural agencies to whose commands and desires we must submit ourselves—is not merely opposed to the humanistic generalities, it condemns them as distractions from our duty. Individual autonomy it describes as pride, a terrible sin because it amounts to repudiation of the deity's authority, a refusal to acknowledge the finite soul's complete dependence upon, and therefore the imperative to submit to, the will of God. That was the crime of Milton's Lucifer: he rejected enslavement to the will—the whim—of God, and asserted instead 'the unconquerable Will / And courage never to submit or yield / To bow and sue for grace with suppliant knee / That were low indeed.'

The quest for knowledge is a dangerous sin too: the first man and woman were forbidden to eat the fruit of the tree of knowledge, and all religions since have censored, burned books (and their authors), and promoted ignorance as a route to salvation. Tolstoy's Levin is an example of someone who embraces the idea that salvation lies in ignorance and simplicity; at the end of *Anna Karenina* he decides to abandon the hard task of seeking philosophical understanding to share the unlettered faith of his peasants. (Dostoevsky perceptively wrote that, given Levin's character, he would never be able to sustain the pretence of this for long; soon after the novel's end, said Dostoevsky, he would 'snag his soul on a rusty nail' and have to start over again.)

Humanist culture, meaning philosophy and science, is (says religion) the folly of the wise that blinds them to their true duty of submission to God. The fellowship of man, in the sense of the political striving for justice in human affairs, is (says religion) likewise a distraction; for a luminous example, consider the medieval church's emphasis on the teaching that we are born to our station in life, and must endure, trusting for justice in what will happen in an after-life. That doctrine might quietly have been shelved in some versions of the faith in its continual process of reinvention that saves it from demise by contempt or desuetude — consider the Church of England giving up the doctrine of Hell in 1920, and the Roman Catholic Church abandoning the doctrine of limbo in the early twenty-first century. But it remains a feature of the solace that the faith offers that the meek and those who mourn and weep will inherit the king-dom, whereas those who enjoy the sunshine of this life might expect an appropriate and less pleasant adjustment in the life to come.

These are some central ways in which the religious out-look contrasts with the humanist outlook, and nothing could be sharper or clearer than the battle-lines thus demar-cated over the great question of the good life for human-kind.

The appeal of religion in the lives of ordinary people has very little to do with its intellectual content, such as it is, except in the vaguest sense that it satisfies the need felt by most for some form of closure or definition in ordinary con-ceptions of things. So each of the questions, 'Why is there a universe?', 'How did it begin?' and 'What is it for?' can all be given the illusion of an answer by invoking a deity and (if that is not enough) the giant fig leaf of the mystery of the deity's intentions and behaviour which we finite minds cannot grasp. Despite the fact that the statement 'the uni-verse was created by God' not only explains nothing, but appears to do so by employing a greater puzzle to solve a lesser, does not trouble many minds.

The appeal of religion is accordingly not intellectual but emotional, and therefore non-rational, so that arguments concerning the irrationality of religious belief avail little. Religion offers something 'higher', something over-arch-ing, something that seems to make sense of things, to organ-ise the inchoate nature of experience and the world into a single framework of apparent meaning. It also offers rituals and routines for dealing with the more significant of life's transitions, from the arrival of a child, to marriage, to death. It offers a crutch in times of fear, despair and grief. It purports to provide a parallel place in life, somewhere to step aside, take stock, and be peaceful for a time; one has only to think of the charm of a country church, very still and musty with an aura of difference from quotidian life and its less exalted urgencies.

For less reflective minds, religion appears to be necessary for morality. The logic of this was once a simple matter: no-one could imagine that anyone could see the point of thinking about morality, and acting on those thoughts, unless there were sanctions of reward and punishment to provide motivation for moral behaviour. Presumably it was incomprehensible to the Church Fathers that an Athenian of the Periclean age could be motivated by a desire to see the good prevail for its own sake, or by a wish to succeed morally as an individual in the light of principles. No, there must be the threat of hell-fire and the promise of bliss to make sense of moral endeavour. A slightly more sophisticated (in both senses) calculation now operates: one obeys the moral injunctions of one's religion out of love for or gratitude to the deity, or out of one's commitment to faith in that deity.

None of the religious grounds for moral endeavour have cogency. Fear of punishment might be a prudential reason for obeying an injunction of some kind, but it is not a logical one. Nor is anticipation of reward. Consider: if I told you not to lie, and you asked why, and I said 'because I will kick you if you do' or alternatively 'because I will give you a banana if you do not', I would not have given you a reason not to lie, only an incentive. As to the claim that we should obey God's will because he loves us, the spuriousness of the idea is well exposed by a similar example: suppose I say, 'I love you therefore jump off that high building', you would not regard my attachment to you as a good reason for jumping off the building. Nor would you if I claimed that your belief in my existence was a reason for you to jump off the building, 'What,' you might legitimately ask in both cases, 'is the connection?' — for of course there is none.

Since these exhaust the supposed bases of religious ethics, it is no surprise that the philosophers of the early modern period returned to discussion of ethical foundations, recognising that if there is a deity and if the deity is good, then its being good is a result of its conforming to moral principles just as a good man does. Bertrand Russell put the point another way in his characteristically succinct manner by observing that not even theologians think that the proposition 'God is good' is a tautology. And to take the alternative tack of claiming that what is good is whatever God says it is, is in effect to claim that might is right, which we know to be false. Serious reflection not only shows, in this way, that religious bases for morality are vacuous, but also the superiority of humanistic approaches. This is because moral striving for a humanist is a matter of trying to understand human nature and the human condition, and on that basis to identify the good for a human being, and to act to bring it about for himself and others. Accordingly humanism does not see the question of what is good as answered — a religion claims it was definitely answered long ago — but rather as the subject of a continuing conversation that mankind has with itself about what matters and what is good as it encounters new challenges and acquires more knowledge and — a greater thing still — more understanding.

Note that the humanist premise does not foreclose discussion about what the good might be; indeed if anything it assumes that it might be a multiple and various thing, according to the natures and choices of individuals, and thus demanding the widest liberty (consistently with the principle of no harm to others) for experiments in the direction of flourishing and achievement in human experience.

Less latitude is appropriate on the question of the response that a humanist must give to religion's claim to provide an overarching sense of meaning to the world, and a space within it for the enjoyment of spiritual satisfactions. Of course it is the illusion of meaning that religion offers, but the psychological reality of its satisfactions is a datum. What does humanism say to these points?

In states of uncertainty and lack of comprehension, people are anxious to have a neat and definite sense of the world they occupy. The great attraction of religion in this respect is that it offers simple closed stories in response. It takes intellectual maturity to live with the open-endedness and uncertainties of science, where the discovery of answers to certain questions is simultaneously the posing of more questions and sometimes greater uncertainties. The unfinished texture of a world-view that proportions theory to evidence, waits on experiment, and is undogmatic and professionally ready to be refuted by countervailing evidence, is hard for the kind of mind that wants everything easy and ready-wrapped. In the world explored by science and philosophy there is no pre-packaged child-friendly pat statement about the meaning of life. On humanism's view, meaning is to be made, not found. It accordingly poses something tougher but deeper than religion in this respect; and asks for harder, more careful work in response.

The question of spiritual satisfaction — the feeding of the hungers of heart and mind — on which religion prides itself is more directly answered. Much of what people do by way of emotional and intellectual refreshment — meeting friends, attending a concert, reading, planting a garden, walking in the country, going on holiday, learning something new, responding to the needs of others — is exactly what is meant by 'seeking and finding spiritual satisfaction', only going under these more mundane names. The most ordinary forms of entertainment and pleasure ease the heart of its everyday concerns, and although no-one chatting in a pub or having a long hot bath would think of dignifying either activity with so ambitious a label, they are in fact spiritual exercises nevertheless. Once people recognise this at first astonishing fact, the belief that such refreshment can only truly be found by signing on to a set of other-worldly commitments ceases to be plausible. The human spirit becomes a feature of what is here present in individual experience, and opportunities for the satisfaction of its needs lie all around, in the fields and the sky and the music on the CD player and the volume of poetry on the bookshelf. It lies in the quest for knowledge, and the work of improving what one can in the world. Above all it lies in relationships, in love and friendship, and in the sense of belonging to the human family.

Religion is a hangover from the infancy of mankind, from the time of ignorance and the fear it causes, and from states of society when the many were coerced by the few. Humanism is the grown-up version of moral consciousness, in which people try to take responsibility for themselves, and acknowledge their responsibility to others. As befits a scheme of thought that suits intellectual immaturity, religious belief persists because its votaries assiduously proselytise the young. No-one is born a Christian or a Muslim, but is made one by social conditioning; a person's religion, for 99.9% of its votaries, is an accident of geography. One thing humanism hopes for is freedom from the perpetuation of the cycle in which each generation indoctrinates the next in its superstitions. The world would be a very different place if this abuse were to end. It would be up to humanists to make sure that it would be a far better place too.

Kenan Malik

Multiculturalism and the Politics of Identity

'The demand is not for inclusion within the fold of "universal humankind" on the basis of shared human attributes', the feminist and sociologist Sonia Kruks has written about identity politics; 'nor is it for respect "in spite of one's differences". Rather, what is demanded is respect for oneself as different.' (Kruks, 2000: 85)

At the heart of contemporary notions of identity is not just a belief in the importance of difference but the idea that difference is important in and of itself. The assertion of difference is viewed as a means of giving people a voice and allowing them to live 'authentic' lives. 'There is a certain way of being human that is *my* way', wrote Charles Taylor in his much-discussed essay on 'The Politics of Recognition'. 'I am called upon to live my life in this way ... Being true to myself means being true to my own originality' (Taylor, 1994: 28).

The belief that people find themselves through voicing their differences with others finds its political expression in multiculturalism. Since an individual's cultural background frames their identity and helps define who they are, multiculturalists argue, so if we want to treat individuals with dignity and respect we must also treat with dignity and respect the groups that furnish them with their sense of personal being. 'The liberal is in theory committed to equal respect for persons', the political philosopher Bhikhu Parekh points out. 'Since human beings are culturally embedded, respect for them entails respect for their cultures and ways of life.' (Parekh, 1994)

The multiculturalist argument provides a direct challenge to a humanist approach. From a humanist perspective what gives people a voice is not the authenticity of their belonging but their existence as political actors. In its traditional Kantian sense, respect requires us to treat every human being equally as a moral, autonomous being. It is in this sense that 'shared human attributes' are important. Every individual possesses the capacity to express political and moral views and to act upon them. And every individual is responsible for their views and actions and is capable of being judged by them. Political voice emerges from the capacity of human beings to act collectively in pursuit of their conscious goals. Identity is an expression not just of our given being – the skin into which we are born, the faith of our parents, the sex with which we enter the world – but also the capacity to make conscious choices that can help transcend our given attributes.

Multiculturalists turn the idea of respect, and the notion of identity, on its head. In demanding 'Respect for oneself as different … *qua* women, *qua* blacks, *qua* lesbians' (Kruks, 2000), multiculturalists celebrate not identities created through conscious action, but identities defined by a set of attributes that, whether rooted in biology, faith or history, are fixed in a certain sense and compel people to act in particular ways. It is telling that Charles Taylor uses the passive voice in suggesting that 'I am called upon to live my life in this way'. Who does the calling? Seemingly the identity itself. For Taylor, identity appears to come first, with the human actor following in its shadow. Or, as the philosopher John Gray has put it, identities are 'a matter of fate, not choice.' (Gray, 2000: 121)

These ideas about culture and identity draw on beliefs that came to the fore towards the end of the eighteenth century largely as part of the Romantic reaction to the Enlightenment. Whereas Enlightenment *philosophes* saw progress as civilisation overcoming the resistance of traditional cultures with their peculiar superstitions, irrational prejudices and outmoded institutions, for the Romantics the steam-roller of progress and modernity was precisely what they feared. Enlightenment *philosophes* tended to see civilisation in the singular. Romantics favoured cultures in the plural. Distinct cultures were not aberrant forms to be destroyed but a precious inheritance to be cherished and protected. For Johann Gottfried Herder, the philosopher who perhaps best articulated the Romantic notion of culture, every people or nation possessed a unique character of its own, a character defined by its *Kultur*: its particular language, literature, history and modes of living. Every culture was authentic in its own terms. And every individual found his authentic voice — and his true identity — by participating in his culture.

All these ideas have filtered down into contemporary discussions of culture and identity. For most multiculturalists, the heterogeneity and diversity that defines contemporary societies, especially in the West, makes old-style equality, rooted in Enlightenment notions of universalism inadequate, even dangerous. The Enlightenment idea that all people flourish best under the same kinds of social institutions and forms of governance are a fantasy because the world is too complex and too varied to be subsumed under a single totalising theory. Universalism is a 'Eurocentric' viewpoint, a means of imposing Euro-American ideas of rationality and objectivity on other peoples. In the place of universal rights come differential rights. 'Justice between groups', as the political philosopher Will Kymlicka has put it, 'requires that members of different groups are accorded different rights' (Kymlicka, 1995: 47).

We cannot treat individuals equally unless groups also treated equally. And since, in the words of Iris Young, 'groups cannot be socially equal unless their specific experience, culture and social contributions are publicly affirmed and recognised', so society must protect and nurture cultures, ensure their flourishing and indeed their survival (Young, 1990). Hence we must make a distinction between what the sociologist Tariq Madood calls the 'equality of individualism' and 'equality encompassing public ethnicity: equality as not having to hide or apologise for one's origins, family or community, but requiring others to show respect for them, and adapt public attitudes and arrangements so that the heritage they represent is encouraged rather than contemptuously expect them to wither away.'(Madood, 1997: 20)

But what does this mean in practice? Should schools, for instance, be compelled to teach Creationism because it is part of Christian fundamentalist culture? Or should public arrangements be adapted to reflect the belief of many cultures that homosexuality is a sin? These are not simply abstract questions. In 2002, in Australia's Northern Territory, Jackie Pascoe Jamilmira, a 50 year-old Aboriginal man, was given a 24-hour prison sentence for assaulting and raping a 15-year-old girl. He had apparently been plying the girl's family with gifts since her birth so that she would become his wife upon coming of age. According to the judge, because the girl was an Aborigine, she 'didn't need protection. She knew what was expected of her. It's very surprising to me he was charged at all.' (Fickling, 2002)

In California, a young Laotian-American woman was abducted from her work at Fresno State University and raped. Her assailant, a Hmong immigrant (one of the boat people who had fled Cambodia and Laos in the final stages of the Vietnam war) explained to the court that this was a customary way of choosing a bride among his tribe. The court agreed that he had to be judged largely by his own cultural standards and sentenced him to just 120 days in jail (Benhabib, 2002: 87).

Most multiculturalists would undoubtedly argue that these cases have little to do with real multicultural policies. Yet it is not difficult to see how the demand that everyone's heritage should be respected and that public arrangements be adapted to preserve each distinct heritage would inevitably create situations such as these. In Australia, courts increasingly accept that Aborigines should have the right to be treated according to their own customs rather than be judged by 'whitefella law'. According to Colin McDonald, a Darwin barrister and expert in customary law, 'Human rights are essentially a creation of the last hundred years. These people have been carrying out their law for thousands of years.' (Fickling, 2002)

This is a central theme to many kinds of multicultural policies — that to preserve cultural authenticity, we must respect the right of certain people to do X because their ancestors also did X. The demand that because a cultural practice has existed for a long time, so it should be preserved, is a modern version of the naturalistic fallacy — the belief that ought derives from is. For nineteenth century social Darwinists, morality — how we ought to behave — derived from the facts of nature — how humans are. This became an argument to justify capitalist exploitation, colonial oppression, racial savagery and even genocide. Today, virtually everyone recognises the falsity of this argument. Yet, when talking of culture rather than of nature, many multiculturalists continue to insist that 'is' defines 'ought'.

Modern multiculturalism seeks self-consciously to yoke people to their identities for their own good, the good of those cultures and the good of society. A clear example is the attempt by the Quebecois authorities to protect French culture. The Quebec government has legislated to forbid French speakers and immigrants from sending their children to English-language schools; to compel businesses with more than fifty employees to be run in French; and to ban English commercial signs. So, if your ancestors were French you, too, must by government fiat speak French whatever your personal wishes may be. Charles Taylor regards this as acceptable because the flourishing and survival of French culture is a good. 'It is not just a matter of having the French language available for those who might choose it', he argues. Quebec is 'making sure that there is a community of people here in the future that will want to avail itself of the opportunity to use the French language.' Its policies 'actively seek to *create* members of the community ... assuring that future generations continue to identify as French-speakers.' (Taylor, 1994: 58-59)

An identity here has become a bit like a private club. Once you join up, you have to abide by the rules. But unlike the

Groucho or the Garrick it's a private club you *must* join. Rather than being an expression of an individual's authentic self, identity can often seem like the denial of individual agency in the name of cultural authenticity.

Take, for instance, the argument put forward by the sociologist Joseph Raz who argues, in common with many multiculturalists, that 'It is in the interest of every person to be fully integrated in a cultural group' (Raz, 1995: 177). But what is to be fully integrated? If a Muslim woman rejects sharia law, is she demonstrating her lack of integration? What about a Jew who doesn't believe in the legitimacy of the Jewish State? Or a French Quebecois who speaks only English? Would Galileo have challenged the authority of the Church if he had been 'fully integrated' into his culture? Or Thomas Paine have supported the French Revolution? Or Salman Rushdie written *The Satanic Verses*? Cultures only change, societies only move forwards because many people, in Kwame Anthony Appiah's words, 'actively resist being fully integrated into a group'. For them 'integration can sound like regulation, even restraint' (Appiah, 2005: 125). Far from giving voice to the voiceless, in other words, the so-called politics of difference appears to undermine individual autonomy, reduce liberty and enforce conformity.

Part of the problem here is a constant slippage in multiculturalism talk between the idea of humans as culture-bearing creatures and the idea that humans have to bear a *particular* culture. Clearly no human can live outside of culture. To say that no human can live outside of culture, however, is not to say they have to live inside a *particular* one. To view humans as culture-bearing is to view them as social beings, and hence as transformative beings. It suggests that humans have the capacity for change, for progress, and for the creation of universal moral and political forms through reason and dialogue. To view humans as having to bear *specific* cultures is, on the contrary, to deny such a capacity for transformation.

The relationship between cultural identity and racial difference becomes even clearer if we look at the argument that cultures must be preserved. For Charles Taylor, once we're concerned with identity, nothing 'is more legitimate than one's aspiration that it is never lost'. Hence a culture needs to be protected not just in the here and now but through 'indefinite future generations' (Taylor, 1994: 40). But what does it mean for a culture to decay? Or for an identity to be lost? Will Kymlicka draws a distinction between the 'existence of a culture' and 'its "character" at any given moment' (Kymlicka, 1995: 104). The character of culture can change but such changes are only acceptable if the existence of that culture is not threatened. But how can a culture exist if that existence is not embodied in its character? By 'character' Kymlicka seems to mean the actuality of a culture: what people do, how they live their lives, the rules and regulations and institutions that frame their existence. So, in making the distinction between character and existence, Kymlicka seems to be suggesting that Jewish, Navajo or French culture is not defined by what Jewish, Navajo or French people are actually doing. For if Jewish culture is simply that which Jewish people do or French culture is simply that which French people do, then cultures could never decay or perish—they would always exist in the activities of people.

So, if a culture is not defined by what its members are doing, what does define it? The only answer can be that it is defined by what its members *should* be doing. And what you should be doing, for cultural preservationists, is what your ancestors were doing. Culture here has become defined by biological descent. And biological descent is a polite way of saying 'race'. As the American writer Walter Benn Michaels puts it, 'In order for a culture to be lost... it must be separable from one's actual behaviour, and in order for it to be separable from one's actual behaviour it must be anchorable in race' (Michaels, 1995: 123).

Once membership of cultural groups is defined by the possession of certain characteristics, and rights and privileges granted by virtue of possessing those characteristics, it is a short step to deny membership to people who do not possess those characteristics and hence to deny them certain

rights and privileges. The language of diversity all too easily slips into the idiom of exclusion. Will Kymlicka suggests
that, 'It is right and proper that the character of a culture
changes as a result of the choices of its members.' But, he
goes on, 'while it is one thing to learn from the larger world',
it is quite another 'to be swamped by it' (Kymlicka, 1995:
104).

What could this mean? That a culture has the right to keep
out members of another culture? That a culture has the right
to prevent its members from speaking another language,
singing non-native songs or reading non-native books?
Kymlicka's warning about 'swamping' should, as Kwame
Appiah has observed, make us sit up and take notice. It is,
after all, the political right that has long exploited fears of
cultural swamping to scapegoat foreigners and restrict
immigration. Will Kymlicka is a liberal anti-racist and certainly no xenophobe. But once it becomes a matter of political principle that cultures should not be swamped by
outsiders, it is difficult to resist such reactionary arguments.
Johann Gottfried Herder, the French philosopher Alain
Finkielkraut observes, has become the cheerleader for both
sides of the political spectrum 'inspiring at the same time ...
unyielding celebrations of ethnic identity and expressions
of respect for foreigners, aggressive outbursts by xeno-
phobes and generous pronouncements by xenophiles'
(Finkielkraut, 1997: 91-92).

What has facilitated such a meeting of minds has been the
narrowing of politics in recent decades. The broad ideologi-
cal divides that characterised politics in the past have been
all but erased and politics has become less about competing
visions of the kinds of society that people want than a
debate about how best to run the existing political system.
As the meaning of politics has become squeezed, so people
have begun to view themselves and their social affiliations
in a different way. Social solidarity has become increasingly
defined not in political terms — as collective action in pursuit of certain political ideals — but in terms of ethnicity or
culture. The question people ask themselves are not so
much 'What kind of society do I want to live in?' as 'Who are

we?'. The first question looks forward for answers and defines them in terms of the common values and actions necessary for social change. The second looks back and seeks answers — and defines identity — in terms of the history and heritage that defines a group as different.

In this process, the very meaning of social justice has become eviscerated. In the brave new world of identity politics, the American sociologist Nancy Fraser has observed, 'The remedy required to redress injustice will be cultural recognition, as opposed to political-economic redistribution' (Fraser, 1993: 75). Don't worry about poverty, inequality and injustice, let's celebrate diversity instead. Far from giving voice to the voiceless, the politics of identity seeks accommodation to a world in which the possibilities of social change appear diminished.

The irony of multiculturalism is that, as a political process, it undermines much of what is valuable about cultural diversity as lived experience. When people say multiculturalism is a good thing what they generally mean is that mass immigration has helped make Britain, for instance, a less inward-looking, more vibrant, more cosmopolitan place. But this does not mean that diversity is good in and of itself. Diversity is important because it allows us to expand our horizons, to compare and contrast different values, beliefs and lifestyles, and make judgements upon them. It is important, in other words, because it allows us to engage in political dialogue and debate that can help create more universal values and beliefs, and a collective language of citizenship. But it is precisely such dialogue and debate, and the making of such judgements, that contemporary multiculturalism attempts to suppress in the name of 'tolerance', 'authenticity' and 'respect'. As humanists we should embrace diversity as lived experience but reject multiculturalism as a political process.

References

Appiah, Kwame Anthony, 2005, *The Ethics of Identity*, Princeton: Princeton University Press

Benhabib, Seyla, 2002, *The Claims of Culture: Equality and Diversity in the Global Era*, Princeton: Princeton University Press

Fickling, David, 2002, 'Bridging whitefella law and clan justice', *Guardian*, 30 December

Finkielkraut, Alain, 1997 (1987) *The Defeat of the Mind*, New York: Columbia University Press

Fraser, Nancy, 1993, 'From Redistribution to Recognition? Dilemmas of justice in a "post-socialist" age', *New Left Review*, 212 July/August

Gray, John, 2000, *Two Faces of Liberalism*, New York: New Press

Kruks, Sonia, 2000, *Retrieving Experience: Subjectivity and Recognition in Feminist Politics* Ithaca, NY: Cornell University Press

Kymlicka, Will, 1995, *Multicultural Citizenship*, Oxford: Oxford University Press

Madood, Tariq, 1997, 'Introduction', in Madood, Tariq and Werbner, Pnina (eds), *The Politics of Multiculturalism in the New Europe*, London: Zed, 1997

Michaels, Walter Benn, 1995, *Our America: Nativism, Modernism and Pluralism*, Durham: Duke University Press

Parekh, Bhikhu, 1994, 'Superior peoples: The narrowness of liberalism from Mill to Rawls', *Times Literary Supplement*, 25 February

Raz, Joseph, 1995, *Ethics in the Public Domain*, Oxford: Oxford University Press

Taylor, Charles, 1994, 'The politics of recognition' in Amy Gutmann (ed) *Multiculturalism: Examining the politics of recognition*, Princeton: Princeton University Press

Young, I, 1990, *Justice and the Politics of Difference*, Princeton: Princeton University Press

Daphne Patai

The Fading Face of Humanism

We are born through separation and live and die alone. Defining ourselves in relation to a world full of other selves, each inescapably aware of its insularity, is a never-ending task. No matter how much we claim to be part of a group, no matter how often we participate in mass demonstrations, parades, boycotts, or petitions, our unique organisms persist, encapsulated by our separate bodies and minds. Whether a million of us are lined up and shot sequentially or vaporised at the same instant, each of us still experiences only our own individual death, even if that death is multiplied one million times. This is the sad and glorious fact of our existence — that we are numerous yet unique, each alone, each an individual self, however profound the links we forge with others through empathy and imagination, made all the more necessary given our fundamental condition. We cannot escape this individuality as long as we still have brains, bodies, and minds.

Why, then, do we see such a resurgence of the phenomenon of identity politics? Why this eagerness to categorise individuals first and foremost as members and defenders of this and that group, embodiments of one or another collective identity, always set in opposition to some other group identity?

Certainly numerous historical examples exist that should have cured us of any enthusiasm for such habits: whites played identity politics when they deprived blacks of their civil rights. And men when they bestowed on women sec-

ond-class status. Hitler did so when he treated Jews as a
virus on the body politic. And the Turks when they slaugh-
tered Armenians. Mao did it when he launched an attack on
intellectuals. The examples — and the body count — go on
and on. Yes, these injuries were done to groups, but they
were experienced by individuals, each one encountering as
a self-conscious entity the fate that was imposed on the
group. With such a tradition, it's hard to imagine that,
today, identity politics could be considered acceptable. Yet
it is the most common game found in our universities, and
has spread from there both up (to the workplace and the
society at large) and down (to primary and secondary education). 'Just desserts,' some might say, but no increase in
the moral and political health of the world. Indeed, identity
politics is considered not only acceptable today but desirable and even obligatory. As if the only progress that has
been made were that of reversal: the first shall be the last,
and the least among you shall have the best claim to …

To what? An interesting question. Minority identity, once
a stigma, is now a badge. A graduate student mocks the few
professors at an elite school who dare express dissatisfac-
tion with his work: 'They can't touch me because I'm
Chicano!' he explains to fellow students. An applicant for
an academic position begins a letter with a statement of
identity: 'I am 1/8 Navajo.' A committee searching for a
'Chinese scholar' in a languages and literatures department
has to clarify whether they are naming a racial identity or a
subject matter — and opts for both. A local writer tries to get
speaking gigs by pitching her work in terms of identity: 'I
am a Jewish lesbian …' A student says in a college literature
class: 'As whites, we shouldn't criticise a black writer's met-
aphors.' Praise and blame; pride and shame. Categories, not
individual selves, appear everywhere we look.

Perhaps it's time to give Samuel Johnson's famous obser-
vation new life by varying just one element: 'Identity politics is the last refuge of a scoundrel'. Given the general
public agreement that self-esteem is crucial for healthy
development, and in light of our species' sorry history of
persecution based on differences among human groups,

how can I hold this view? Because (as that sorry history impresses upon us) only a recognition of our common humanity — rooted in an inescapable individuality, to which, however, we can bring our uniquely human qualities of empathy, imagination, and mutual recognition - provides a lasting basis for building a just society. By contrast, identity politics today is always an invitation to extortion or to exculpation, as the wearisome struggle that Noretta Koertge and I have called 'the oppression sweepstakes' amply demonstrates (Patai and Koertge, 2003).

In higher education, the new grievance studies bring with them the decline of free speech, as schools devise 'harassment policies' that treat speech as verbal action and name those identity groups that are to be protected from unpleasantness. Recently, for example, Harvard University added 'gender identity' to its anti-harassment policies, in view of complaints by transgendered students. This move (made also by dozens of other universities) attracted the attention of civil liberties attorney Harvey Silverglate, co-founder of FIRE, the Foundation for Individual Rights in Education. (I am on the board of directors of this organisation, which is a non-partisan defender of First Amendment rights in higher education.) Silverglate sent a letter to Harvard's General Counsel:

> I read in yesterday's Harvard Crimson that the university has finally taken the giant step of making Harvard 'safe' for trans-gendered students, much as it has in the past made it so 'safe' for so many sub-groups of humanity that it is no longer safe even to speak one's mind on the campus lest an errant thought offend a member of a protected group. Ah, progress! ...
>
> ... This alum suggests that the University get rid of all of its ridiculous 'civil rights' policies, which are very harmful in that they keep dividing and sub-dividing humanity into ever smaller and ever-more-contentious sub-groups and then restore 'rights' to these groups by punishing the speech of all.

Silverglate suggested that Harvard supplant all its current 'civil rights' codes with one simple statement, as follows:

> Harvard being a meritocracy, it is hereby declared a viola-
> tion of university policy to deprive any student of any ben-
> efits offered by the university, or to punish or disadvantage
> any student, on the basis of any factor or condition that is
> not rationally related to the student's abilities and demon-
> strated character.
> (email to Robert Iuliano, 13 April 2006; reprinted by per-
> mission)

Although he does not use the term 'humanism,'
Silverglate's criticism obviously rests on precisely such a
concept, in opposition to the identity politics that currently
prevail. In the absence of a broad commitment to humanism, instead of defending the inalienable rights we possess
as human beings, we are explained, and explained away, by
our supposed identities, even as these constantly shift in
response to newly emerging identity groups.

Two important ingredients in the rise of identity groups
—both of them inimical to humanism—are the dogma of
social constructionism and the rhetoric of postmodernism.
Social constructionism insists on the man-made status of all
significant aspects of our being, while postmodernism provides a fashionable lexicon that sounds sophisticated as it
undermines any and all claims about humans as a collec-
tivity. Both are used opportunistically, forcing biology (and
with it a common humanity) to disappear from view, reason as a characteristic of the species to be undermined, and
appeals to logic and empirical evidence to be cast aside as
mere verbal tropes. A currently popular example is the
insistence by many feminists in the academy that heterosex-
uality is a social construct, not rooted in biology, and that
even sexual dimorphism is a social, not a biological fact.
What is gained by such a stance? It bores away at our common biology, at what we all share, and at the same time provides a delusion of control over all aspects of our world—
thus seeming to justify any particular group's political
demands while giving them grounds for permanent gripes
against others. All sorts of inconvenient facts can be challenged (or, better yet, 'interrogated') by such strategies.
To argue that biology plays a role in human affairs, for
example, is tantamount to being hopelessly in thrall to

notions of scientific objectivity rendered obsolete by postmodernism.

If one wishes to criticise some ideas using minimal energy, and those ideas happen to belong to your opponents, what better weapon is there than to insist that all ideas are equally vulnerable and reflect group interests? Or that truth is nothing more than one person's (or group's) narrative? Of course, such claims are typically applied to others' views, not one's own. Mere assertion replaces argumentation, and, however well-based the ideas of one's opponents, they can be readily dismissed as an expression of their political interests.

So we see critical legal theorists argue that the First Amendment protects the interests of privileged white men, whose speech is damaging to women. And black scholars now make the same argument about 'white' law generally. Though no one can adhere to such claims with any consistency (since they are self-refuting), the rhetoric goes on. To admit that there is reason, empirical evidence, and knowledge that are not just the opinions of a group is dangerous. For might one's own views not be subjected to as severe a scrutiny as anyone else's? And what would happen if truth could not easily be dismissed as 'truth'? Today, even lawyers can be found parroting such notions as they defend a particular client.

Far more convenient, of course, to dismiss an idea because of the identity of its proponents (the 'genetic fallacy'), and to suggest that challenges to this procedure are evidence of racism, sexism, heterosexism, or one of the many other –isms floating around ready to replace reflection. One result of this habit is an atmosphere in which who-says-what comes to have extraordinary weight as people on all sides abdicate a commitment to reasoned discourse and investigation of facts. 'Facts,' I ought to write. For they too are now nothing more than the expression of the notions of an identity group. In the absence of a commitment to the pursuit of knowledge not made subservient to politics, identity politics steps in, hastening to adjudicate among competing knowledge claims.

Humanism, by contrast, would impose a far higher standard on us all — the standard of rationality and fairness. As John Searle writes, in his defense of rules of investigation (against the mere assertions favored by punsters such as Derrida): '[I]t is not enough to say "I call that distinction into question." You actually have to have an argument' (Searle, 2005). And the problem with arguments, alas, is that they need to be judged according to norms of argumentation — norms that do not, and should not, include who-said-what, how fervently someone holds to an idea, or whether that idea reinforces his or her own interests. But to grant this is to adhere to a standard by which mere identity would not be a decisive factor — and this would disempower people hoping to pressure others into going along with them on the basis of supposed past guilt and blame.

Frank Furedi writes, in his essay in this volume, that humanism stresses 'subjectivity' — which may at first glance appear to undermine identity politics. But subjectivity, too, is vulnerable to all the abuses derived from claims about group suffering. Feelings untempered by reason, impervious to investigation, and refusing to be moderated by contrary evidence, are a danger all too common at the present time. Sincere feelings are no doubt even worse than just plain feelings, since the latter may be held more lightly and hence be more amenable to change.

Unlike Furedi, who is worried about the way ideas about nature can strengthen determinism, I, coming from feminist debates and academic orthodoxies, see quite a different danger: that of promoting the determinism of social constructionism, with its corollary that nothing is impervious to our political programmes. Most universities in the United States today are secular institutions and the recent demand of fundamentalists to impose Creationism in the classroom will never take hold as long as academic freedom and a commitment to reason prevail. But many academics today are not in a good position to mount such a defence, for they have themselves engaged in attacks on science, and on the very notion of objectivity. AC Grayling, also in this volume, like Furedi, embraces humanism because of its challenge to religious ideas. But, again, what strikes me at the present time is that identical terms can now bolster either left or right positions. Both Creationists and feminists can deride science and its influence. Both can get mileage out of challenging reason and knowledge. And who but the sex traditionally dismissed as distant from rational thought — women, that is — is today staking out its claim for a special kind of 'knowing' as a proper corrective to the tyranny of patriarchal reasoning? Politics indeed makes for strange bedfellows.

Furedi worries about 'environmental determinism' and sees human subjectivity in danger of being pushed aside as emphasis falls on impersonal forces. But, I would respond, the danger is equally great from those who would stress subjectivity and deny the role of biology in human affairs. Why one would want to engage in such a denial is a complex question: some scholars have stressed the assault on our egos that occurs when we are forced to see ourselves as animals, like other animals. And so, to counter this assault, we insist on social constructionism, which sees not nature but nurture as the key ingredient in making us what we are. Such views today have taken on the status of dogma in women's studies and many other politically-motivated programmes in colleges and universities.

The danger, it seems to me, for students coming out of humanities and social science programmes these days, is not so much that they are likely to see humans as irretrievably linked to nature (and thus deprived of agency), but the contrary one: of seeing human beings as having no links to nature, no underlying conditions of existence. For into that vacuum drive those with the most ruthless political will. While this may seem like an absurdity (and I think it is), for the reasons Furedi outlines, it makes sense for soi-disant progressives (including feminists) to attack views that treat human beings as being in some sense rooted in nature. Obviously this undermines programmes for change, or at the very least limits the parameters of that change.

It is easy to demonstrate that scepticism toward received ideas is a good thing, and that, for example, a commitment to cultural relativism may lead to efforts to understand cultural differences, to criticisms of one's own culture, to a flexibility in one's mental style and a drawing away from absolute judgments. But these qualities can with surprising ease also turn into defects. When all knowledge claims are seen as situational and interested, what will prevent fundamentalists of various types from imposing their views? All those who have played identity politics now will be in a poor position to challenge on universal grounds views damaging to them — regardless of how ill- or well-founded those views are.

Thus, I want to stress not the secular underpinnings of humanism — as important as I recognise these to be — but rather the universal aspiration of humanism. I cannot imagine a humanist saying: 'Slavery is bad in the Western world, but who are we to criticise it in Africa or Asia?' And yet something very like this is frequent these days. Western societies, we are told, are still deeply in thrall to the Patriarchy; are inherently racist and homophobic, and are a danger to the world; while, say, Muslim societies — well, we mustn't criticise them because to do so is Eurocentric and Orientalist.

If humanism is based on reason, then it stands in stark contradiction to any system of thought that deplores reason, dismisses it as a Western imposition, and opts instead for 'local knowledges.' Whatever the motivation, it is no better to dismiss reason as a creature of 'patriarchy' than to dismiss it as contravening the will of God or Allah. Identity politics demands special status not by virtue of fundamental human rights (which necessarily must be based on something other than distinct national, racial, sexual, or other identities) but of grievances. Yet, ironically, it counts on others to respond in a humanistic way — with concern for individual welfare based on human commonality. Without such an underlying ethos, identity politics could not function in a democratic and liberal society, for it would reduce to nothing more than a violent struggle between and among groups. That such a physical battle does not often take place, for example, in the United States in recent decades is because of the assent given by non-group members to the claims of an oppressed or formerly oppressed group. In other words, other human beings can be relied on to see beyond their group interests, to exercise empathy and imagination, and thus be led to support actions based on general humanistic commitments rather than narrow identity politics.

But such assent is always provisional, depending on particular historical conditions. And a tacit awareness of this short-lived largesse explains why identity groups invariably pursue a the-worse-the-better strategy: it's the only way they can continue to gain a semblance of legitimacy for their claims on others' attention. Still, such claims are always contradictory. Advocates for feminism or for blacks or for gay rights begin by demanding that attention be paid to their claims and grievances and soon enough (as I have seen repeatedly in academic settings) move on to complaints about having to educate others. Why should we, they say, be obliged to spend our time educating others? We're tired of doing this; they should take responsibility for educating themselves about our issues. Failure to do so is merely another way of oppressing us and excluding us.

And these demands, in turn, contribute to an atmosphere of hypervigilance, in which everyone is on the lookout for what state of consciousness-raising and commitment everyone else has achieved. And so we find ourselves back to praise and blame, abject apologies and hidden resentments, distortions and hyperbole, as individuals sort themselves into the identity categories that carry the most weight at the moment and play out the oppression sweepstakes as if it leads to a better world rather than merely to more group conflict.

In the end, those of us who have most enjoyed the benefits of the Western humanist tradition must be the ones to defend it, for it is in our own consciousness that we have encountered its strengths: humanism is universal in scope, founded on respect for the individual, reasoned discourse rather than violence, evidence instead of dogma, and self-correction in place of doctrinaire rigidity.

References

Patai, Daphne and Koertge, Noretta, 2003, *Professing Feminism: Education and Indoctrination in Women's Studies*. Lexington Books (Expanded edition of our 1994 book *Professing Feminism: Cautionary Tales from the Strange World of Women's Studies*. BasicBooks: A New Republic Book.)

Searle, John R, 2005, 'Literary Theory and Its Discontents', in Daphne Patai and Will H Corral (eds) *Theory's Empire: An Anthology of Dissent*. Columbia University Press.

Andrew Copson

Humanism and Faith Schools

Over the twentieth century the UK secularised fast. Church of England baptisms decreased from 55.4% of all babies born in 1960 to 26.5% of babies born in 2002. Since 1992, there have been more civil marriage ceremonies in England and Wales than religious ceremonies and in 2003 they accounted for 68% of all marriages. Of 16 to 34 year olds in Great Britain, almost a quarter (23%) said in 2001 that they had no religion compared with less than 5% of people aged 65 or over. (The data gathered on religion in the 2001 census is in fact generally acknowledged to have given, through bad phrasing of the question, an exaggeratedly high percentage of religious people. A DfES report (Parks et al, 2004), found 65% of children of secondary school age were not religious.) Research by academics such as David Voas (2005) has shown these bald statistics to embody a trend of progressive secularisation from generation to generation and there is no reason, in spite of the growing vociferousness and political activity of some religious individuals and groups, to think that this secularising trend is seeing any reversal in the twenty-first century. Our young people today are one of the least religious generations in Europe, and research published by the Church of England itself suggests that not only are they not religious, they are quite happy being so. As *The Times* reported, summarising the findings:

> Nevertheless, young people do not feel disenchanted, lost
> or alienated in a meaningless world. 'Instead, the data indi-

cated that they found meaning and significance in the reality of everyday life, which the popular arts helped them to
understand and imbibe.' Their creed could be defined as:
'This world, and all life in it, is meaningful as it is,' translated as: 'There is no need to posit ultimate significance
elsewhere beyond the immediate experience of everyday
life'. The goal in life of young people was happiness
achieved primarily through the family. (*The Times*, 8 May
2006)

Faced with this image of 'Generation Y', a horrified Arch-
bishop of York observed that, 'The research suggests young
people are happy with life as it is, that they have felt no need
for a transcendent something else and regard the Church as
boring and irrelevant.' (*The Times*, 8 May 2006) This, apparently, is a problem. That it can be seen as such betrays an
odd fact about our secular society and one that humanists
entering the education debate are forced to keep in mind.

Although the UK secularised fast in the twentieth century
to little obvious ill-effect, there still remains a strong sense
(evident, for example, within the current Government) that
faith equals values and that the non-religious must be
somehow lacking. Humanist values or liberal values – the
values that underpin much of modern education – seem not
to count as values at all. The Australian creationist John
Mackay, visiting Britain in 2006, put it as no British observer
has: 'Parents know that if you try to run a school where the
moral structure is based on humanist, agnostic principles,
then there are no morals at that school' (*Independent*, 18 May
2006). But that same message, though less strident, lies
behind the speeches and remarks of many British politicians when they speak of faith schools.

Of course humanists must, as we always have, involve
ourselves in every aspect of education. We must stand
against relativism and for universal values in an open society, modelled in our schools. The space allowed in this brief
chapter makes it impossible to sketch out a total system of
such schools but one aspect of the wider debate that must be
addressed is the topical question of faith schools. (See BHA,
2006, for a more in depth treatment.) The positive myths
that are perpetuated about faith schools and which allow

government to endorse and encourage their existence and expansion must be exposed and countered if a proper debate around education in purely humanist terms can be supported. Such an exercise is not purely negative – every objection to be made to faith schools has a positive corollary – and it can point the way to a brighter and a more humanised future for our schools and for our young people.

The most often repeated defence of faith schools and one which is implicit in most other defences of them is that faith schools are successful because they are *faith* schools. As Education Secretary, David Blunkett said he wished he could bottle their magic, presumably to share it out with the less fortunate community schools. This 'it's magic' analysis of the situation, however, doesn't fit the facts. Not all faith schools are successful and faith schools that aren't struggle and sink in the league tables just like any struggling school and (just like any struggling school) sometimes they close as a result. Yet when these schools struggle and close, you won't hear the Education Secretary locating the blame in their faith-based ethos and values. Why then is it the religious character of a school that gets the credit when that school succeeds? There is no research to be found that equates religious belief with intelligence, so we can hardly assume that it is because of their presumed religion that children do well academically. And if there is no universally magic faith-based ingredient, how can we explain the higher examination results that faith schools do achieve overall?

For many church schools, the answer has been given by research into these schools' intakes. Faith schools overall take fewer children with special educational needs at both primary and secondary levels and more importantly, research shows that, even though voluntary-aided church schools are ostensibly selecting only on grounds of faith, the effect is to skew the social intake of the school in favour of the affluent and the ambitious (see www.humanism.org.uk for a record of such research). Church schools that perform well become the favourite schools of selective parents and a cycle of selection and achievement can come to exist that (obviously) owes nothing to religion. As Dr Sandie Schagen, Principal Research Officer at the National Foundation for Educational Research, told parliamentarians in 2003:

> On the basis of our research, looking exclusively at achievement, there is not any evidence at all to suggest that increasing the number of faith schools will improve the level of achievement ... Our finding is that basically, when you apply value-added analysis, that advantage all but disappears, which suggests that the difference is based on intake ... you can hypothesise that if they do have better ethos and better behaviour and so on that would lead to better achievement, but we did not find any evidence that that is so. (House of Commons Education and Skills Committee, 2003)

In the case of faith schools from other religions, apparently high achievement is likewise explicable in other ways. Much was made of the fact that the school achieving the most value-added at GCSE in 2005 was a Muslim girls' school, and the familiar arguments for the academic superiority of faith schools were trotted out once more. Closer examination, however, revealed that the cohort of GCSE students numbered only six — an enviably small class size with which even the lowliest community school teacher could presumably achieve great things. In any case, even all this data only measures examination results; there are some indicators where faith schools are outdone by community schools (for example, a higher percentage of non-faith schools were judged 'highly effective' by Ofsted in 2004/5 than faith schools).

So much for the claim of faith schools to academic superiority by virtue of their religious character. But the defender of faith schools at this point moves swiftly on to what he thinks is much more solid ground. So maybe the religious ethos of faith schools cannot account for their apparent academic success, but if there's one thing faith schools do impart, it's values. Values and ethos are something that the community school apparently has no claim on. Lord Adonis was willing to overlook the fact that the A-level results of Catholic schools were lower than the national average when he spoke to the Catholic Education Service, remarking in compensation, 'Your schools are strong on ethos; unashamed about propagating values as well as standards.' (Speech to CES, 18 May 2006) From Prime Minister to successive Labour Education Secretaries, the argument that faith schools are distinctive because of their ethos and values has been repeatedly made. Again, the analysis doesn't fit the facts. There are plenty of community schools that are rated highly for ethos. Just one example is Plashet School in East Ham, London. Ofsted praised the 'outstanding ethos' of this school, which 'values and respects everyone,' and contains children from many different backgrounds; it gets excellent Ofsted reports for social, moral, spiritual and cultural education. It is never sufficient to argue purely from anecdote, but there are many other community schools that can boast the same achievement as Plashet, and even a few examples are enough to give the lie to a view of faith schools as the only transmitters of values.

Quite apart from these proofs of excellent ethos within community schools, we must ask what is so good about the values that faith schools claim to be purveying in any case. We should expect our state-funded schools, the institutions that embody the aspiration of universal education, to embody shared and universal values. But in our secular society, the Church of England (2005) advises that their schools convey to their pupils the fact that a secular view of life is 'ultimately sterile' and gives the purpose of its schools as being to 'Nourish those of the faith; Encourage those of other faiths; Challenge those who have no faith'. Not only is an irrational hierarchy of beliefs apparent here, but it is one that places the majority of young people right at the bottom, apparently more needy than their religious peers of being 'challenged'. Nor is the Church of England unique in its attitude. Ibrahim Lawson, headmaster of the Nottingham Islamia school, speaking on BBC Radio 4, stated that 'the essential purpose of the Islamia school, as with all Islamic schools, is to inculcate profound religious belief in the children.' We must question whether this inculcation of religion can ever be acceptable at public expense because we must question whether these are the sort of 'values' that it is best for our children to be tutored in. The United Nation's Convention on the Rights of the Child states that children in education have the right to 'to seek, receive and impart information and ideas of all kinds ...' and be prepared for 'responsible life in a free society, in the spirit of understanding, peace, tolerance, equality of sexes, and friendship among all peoples, ethnic, national and religious groups ...' and these are the values that should lie at the heart of any school because they recognise what is true – that the child is not a possession of his parents or the state, but an individual with rights accruing to him naturally as he grows and develops (see Law, 2006, for an excellent defence of such liberal education).

Defenders of faith schools, when questioned as to whether this transmission of religion at public expense is legitimate, often point to the fact that faith schools cannot be teaching so extreme a curriculum because, in the state sector, they are required to follow the national curriculum. This defence was used by government to commend the policy of bringing otherwise under-regulated independent faith schools into the state sector, and is true as far as it goes. But the subjects that should concern us most in faith schools – subjects like sex and relationships education, or religious education, aren't on the national curriculum and there is no objective national standard in them to which to hold faith schools. So, whereas community schools have to teach RE that is generally broad and balanced, allowing for critical approaches and the growth of mutual understanding, faith schools can teach whatever they like in their RE lessons – there is no curriculum they are obliged to follow. RE is not perfect in community schools, and humanists have always thought that it needs extensive reform, but in a good community school, RE is more genuinely educational and appropriate to a diverse society than in faith schools.

Nor is it just in the sphere of values, moral or ethical education that it can be wrong to teach only one religious view to children. Creationism (which has been much debated in light of claims that academies funded by evangelical Christians are teaching it in science, or as science), even when taught as true only in RE in faith schools can be damaging. If children are taught the facts of the matter in national curriculum science, and an untrue world-picture in another class, they will realise that the two are incompatible. Although it is bad enough to think they may choose to believe the untrue myth, it is even worse to think that exposure to what are being sold as two different 'truths' may lead the child into the sort of relativism that so many religious representatives are encouraging today.

In contrast to the advocates of a resurgent religiosity in our school system, humanists need to reclaim the values that really do underpin education in this country. Education is the means by which civilisation is transmitted, minds are opened, and young people are prepared for life in the society of which they will be a part. That society will continue, as we observed at the outset of this essay, to become more and more secular, and our education system needs to endorse universal values and humanist principles as the only possible basis for a cohesive society in the future. Schools with a religious ethos, values education that continues to promote a solely religious basis for morality, and a pedagogy that cultivates relativism and undermines truth will not ensure this.

Quite apart from the educational arguments against faith schools, we also face the possibility that an expansion of the sector (especially insofar as it brings ethnic minority religions into the system) also holds out a future of segregation. If the children of Hindu and humanist, Jewish and Muslim parents do not mix in the classroom, and their parents do not mix at the school gate, when will they encounter each other? How will they learn from and about each other if not in a school that models the wider society they must grow up in? And what will the effect of this mutual dislocation turn out to be? A recent ESRC study of young people's civic action (and inaction) gives us a hint of what schools divided along religious lines will produce. It identifies one category of young people as 'Own Group Identified': 'Those who are high on this profile identify strongly with their religion ...

[and] are least interested in environmental issues. They are also less likely to vote, now or in the future , or to take part in demonstrations. They have the lowest rate of participation in recent community and political activities ...' (Haste, 2005: 25).

Organised Humanism in Britain has always prioritised education, and individual humanists such as Sir Bernard Crick have been in the forefront of such recent developments as statutory Citizenship education. The British Humanist Association, in the decade following its own establishment moved to found the Social Morality Council (now the Norham Foundation), and worked constructively with people from Christian and other traditions to seek out common solutions to moral and social problems, despite the obvious differences in matters of fundamental belief that seemed to divide us. It was a co-founder of the Values Education Council, a similarly co-operative body, and has been active for many years in the Religious Education Council and the Sex Education Forum, with individual humanists involved at a local level on committees responsible for RE and in educational projects of dialogue locally.

This humanist approach to education, of collaboration with those adhering to different worldviews, of commitment to the ideal of an open society that should be modelled in schools as much as in the wider community they serve, and the humanistic approach that sees the child as a person with rights and responsibilities that accrue to him as he grows and develops, has much to offer to the contemporary education debate. But is the voice of humanism being granted the attention it deserves? We can claim to have been influential in a number of ways — encouraging reform of RE and the development of statutory citizenship education, and most of all, keeping the issue of 'faith' schools on the agenda, politically and amongst the general public. But the positive message of humanistic education as a values-rich, inclusive and *preferable* model, is still ours to convey.

When a politician praises the faith school he is implicitly deriding the community school. When he waxes lyrical about the ethos and values of the religious institution, he is taking a swipe at the more liberal and humanist pedagogy of our shared institutions. But these institutions, reformed and revitalised, are what are needed in our secular society more than anything. If we cannot find a way to gain a wider recognition of this fact in the century to come, and develop a secular framework for values education that is robust and coherent, we must question whether it is even worth debating humanism at all.[1]

References

BHA, 2006 (2002), *A Better Way Forward*, British Humanist Association (http://www.humanism.org.uk/site/cms/contentViewArticle.asp?article=1589)

Church of England (2005), *Excellence and Distinctiveness: Guidance on RE in Church of England Schools*

House of Commons Education and Skills Committee, 2003, *Secondary Education: Diversity of Provision*, Fourth Report, 22 May http://www.publications.parliament.uk/pa/cm200203/cmselect/cmeduski/94/9402.htm

Parks, A, Phillips, M and Johnson, M, 2004, *Young People in Britain: The Attitudes and Experiences of 12-19 Year Olds*, DfES

Voas, D and Crockett, A, 2005, 'Religion in Britain: Neither Believing nor Belonging', *Sociology*, 39(1):11-28

Law, Stephen, 2006, *The War for Children's Minds*, Routledge

Haste, Helen, 2005, *My voice, my vote, my community*, Nestlé Social Research Programme

1   Thanks are due to Marilyn Mason, David Pollock and Hanne Stinson, on whose work for the British Humanist Association much of this article draws.

Dennis Hayes

Re-humanising Education

Today's obsession with innovations and fads in education obscures the fact that intellectual culture has traditionally been central to our concept of what it is to be human. This is something that is no longer obvious or to be taken for granted. We need to remind ourselves of what Michael Oakeshott stated most succinctly, that: 'Every Human being is born an heir to an inheritance' and to enter this common inheritance of human achievements through education is 'the only way of becoming a human being, and to inhabit it is to be a human being' (Oakeshott, 1973: 158). Not to inhabit it is, of course, to be less than human. One of the greatest challenges facing humanists, then, is recovering and developing not just a particular vision of education, but *the very idea of education*.

What lies behind the collapse of the idea of education is a broader social phenomenon. To wish to educate future generations requires that we still have confidence in human potential and, if we lack that confidence, we will not have confidence to educate our children. Murray Bookchin identified the problem over a decade ago when suggested that society was suffering from a 'sweeping failure of nerve ... a deep-seated cultural malaise that reflects a waning belief in our species' creative abilities. In a very real sense, we seam to be afraid of ourselves—of our uniquely human attributes. We seem to be suffering from a decline in human self-confidence and our ability to create ethically meaningful lives that enrich humanity and the non-human world (Bookchin, 1995: 1).

This decline in human self-confidence is nowhere more apparent than in education, but for all the raging discussion and debate about education and the shortcomings of the current system, the nature and profundity of the problem is rarely acknowledged.

The loss of belief in education

The few critics there are of the educational *content* of current British education policies and proposals reveal a consciousness of a crisis in educational thought but not of its profundity. The critics usually discuss three problems: firstly the absence of a serious consideration of or interest in values, secondly the government's control of the terms of the educational debate, and thirdly a restricted view of the nature of education. One exception is the *Nuffield Review of 14-19 Education* (2004-05) which goes a little further and discusses the wider loss of purpose in education itself. The authors argue that 'Government policy documents on 14-19 have largely failed to articulate underlying aims. There needs to be a constant appraisal of the values which are embedded in educational language and practice and which shape learning experience.' The authors' concern is that more needs to be said about educational aims because 'They reflect the kind of life that is thought to be worth living, the personal qualities worth developing and the sort of society worth creating' (Nuffield, 2005: 24-25). What the review said of 14-19 education can be said of all educational policies.

The problem is that the review's critique is made within an historical framework that no longer applies. Instead of a crisis *in* education, as implied in the review, there is today a crisis *of* education, stemming from the disintegration of the very idea of education. An example of this misdiagnosis is the review's criticism of the false dichotomy between 'academic' and 'vocational' education. The idea behind this dichotomy was always that some or all working class children are not capable of 'academic' education. This can take

radical or 'left-wing' forms, arguing for the value of working class or personal 'knowledge' rather than 'elite' knowledge, or it can be merely an expression of a reactionary and
'right-wing' conservative forms, viewing the working class
as barely civilised and incapable of learning difficult subjects, that is to say, viewing them as barely *human*. The loss
of belief in education, however, academic or otherwise,
means this debate now has no meaning, and the review's
critique is redundant. Government has given up thinking
about what education means because it no longer believes
in it, and yet cannot articulate the diminished and
dehumanising idea that lies behind this abandonment of
education — that no child or young person is capable of education as it was once understood. A prejudice that once
applied to the lower classes now applies to everyone: we are
all seen as barely human.

A humanist concept of education

The humanist ideal of education goes back to the early
grammar schools, and developed through the renaissance
with the introduction of new subjects, particularly mathematics and science. In the 1960s Paul Hirst gave expression
to the idea of a liberal education as embodying initiation
into what he called the distinctive 'forms of knowledge'
with their own particular concepts, logical structures, and
ways of being tested against experience. They are: mathematics, physical sciences, human sciences, history, religion,
literature and art, moral knowledge and philosophy (Hirst,
1973). These are differentiated from 'fields of knowledge',
such as geography, which draw on the various forms. He
gave what was really a proposal for a school curriculum,
and both the subjects and the separate nature of his 'forms
of knowledge' are contested (O'Hear, 1981; Cooper, 1993).

Is 'religion', for example, really a form of knowledge? In
recent years Hirst has revisited his work and has gone along
with current fashion and criticised his earlier approach as
too 'rationalistic' (Hirst, 1993). This debate is worth remembering, not to resolve the contested issues for all time, but

because, whatever view of the 'forms of knowledge' you have, this was at least a debate about the nature of *education*.

Similarly, the original idea of comprehensive education was the culmination of the idea, embodied in the traditional grammar school, that all children are capable of becoming fully human by gaining knowledge of the range of subjects that constituted a liberal education. The idea of a comprehensive education embodied the humanist ideal that everyone could benefit from the acquisition of knowledge. This ideal was a challenge to the idea that the working class, or women, or black and ethic minority groups were not capable of being educated to the highest levels. Whatever social, genetic, cultural or psychological arguments were constructed or devised to show failings and barriers to the acquisition of knowledge, they were mostly thinly disguised exercises in prejudice that made little headway against the idea that every human being had such potential, and that its frustration was the result of social prejudice and discrimination.

This idea, which is the *modern* and not a 'traditional' or 'old' idea of liberal education, has now been lost. Educationalists and teachers see children as incapable of a humanistic education because they no longer believe in humanity. Seeing people as incapable of education is in fact *to see them as less than human*. There is no point in offering an education you don't believe in to children who cannot benefit from it. This philosophy embodies such a diminished view of human potential that it cannot be made explicit, however. Policy makers and politicians cannot argue for a philosophy of education that celebrates a diminished human being. So how is this philosophy expressed?

Education by Examples

Kant said that 'examples are ... the go-cart of judgment' (Kant, 1978: 178) but they are more important in this case. It is from examples rather than from the rhetoric of policy documents that we can extract the unarticulated vision that governing elites and policy wonks have of children and young people. There are two forms of example that are relevant here. Firstly, there are examples of initiatives that have gained popularity with government and educationalists. Secondly, there are examples, given usually in boxed inserts or in the appendices of reports, of educational biographies of individual young people. There is space for just a few, but the methodology of examination by examples is there for everyone to use in this way: ask of any educational initiative — whether a new government policy, an innovation, or an example of a child or young person learning — 'What vision of a child or young person, of a human being, does this initiative express?' It is my contention that they will express a diminished sense of what it is to be human.

Personalised Learning

'Personalised Learning' is the latest buzz phrase, all the rage and interpreted in many different ways (see Johnson, 2004; Leadbeater, 2004; NCSL, 2004; Pollard & James, 2004). The point I want to make is a simple one: the more learning is 'personalised' the less is it educational. It is also in relation to 'Personalised Learning' that we find clear examples of the sort of young people the policy makers have in mind as indicative of humanity. Consider this example:

> James is 15. He was born a heroin addict. His mother is a heroin addict. During James's childhood his father and brother spent most of their time in prison. James rarely attended school, he wasn't interested in learning. Through the intervention of a Drugs Action Team and a voluntary organisation for children a 'learning manager' worked closely with James, finding out what he wanted to do and allowing him to participate in decisions about what he studied. Now his methadone dosage is going down, he's making new friends, he's back in school and his relationship with his mother is better than it was. James had met a network that supported him as an active informed participant in a process that no school alone could have delivered.

Such examples express a pathetic picture of humanity and they are ubiquitous. They present young people as hopeless potential drug users, alcohol abusers, or self abusers, but most importantly as people who are what they are, and who are only motivated to learn what is relevant to their personal lives and existing interests. Policy making based on this view of young people rejects a defining feature of education – its *disinterestedness*. Education is about moving beyond narrow personal and social concerns and problems and gaining knowledge and clarity. The confused plans for 'personalised learning' threaten to put an end to anything that could be called 'education' by depriving 'learners' of the possibility of transforming themselves.

Learning Styles

While 'personalised learning' replaces 'education' with the more general and subjective concept of 'learning', another fashionable approach goes further and suggests children are only capable of learning in certain ways because of their 'learning styles'. The identification of learning styles using various instruments is an industry. A recent study shows 13 of them to have serious flaws (Coffield et al, 2004a and 2004b). Many of the diagnostic instruments examined are neither valid nor reliable. A good number are also conceptually flawed and not properly subject to empirical tests. A further, less technical but more pertinent criticism made in the surveys is that the notion of a 'learning style' is decontextualised from subject knowledge (Coffield et al, 2004b: 60). This seems to me to be decisive. What determines acquisition of knowledge is a matter of learning the logic of subjects rather than anything else.

Unfortunately, the interest in learning styles has not been buried by this study, and teachers can be found sifting the research for the least flawed models to use, while government promotes their use in every subject area. The consequences are frightening. I have been in one school where the pupils had labels on their desks indicating their learning styles 'I'm a kinaesthetic learner', 'I'm an active experimenter' and so on. But the notion of someone having a 'learning style' suggests that their nature is fixed. Thinking of children and young people as being defined by 'learning styles' is just another way of doing them down, of setting limits to their potential.

Emotional Intelligence

Even more popular is the idea that one of the main challenges for education is to develop children and young people's 'emotional intelligence'. The books of Daniel Goleman have been very influential here, not because they are scientific, but because they offer what seems to be a way out of 'emotional ineptitude, desperation, and recklessness in our families our communities and our collective lives' (Goleman 1996: x). What Goleman offers, despite drawing on contested scientific research, is a moralistic way out of what he sees as an emotional malaise towards self restraint and compassion. We need to tutor those animal emotions that lead to violence and gun crime. At a recent meeting organised by the Training and Development Agency for schools I heard teacher after teacher and teacher trainer argue that emotional development was the most important challenge in education. To play with the subtitle of Goleman's best seller, EQ now matters more than IQ.

Behind the rhetoric of excellence and 'education, education, education', these examples reveal a diminished view of what children and young people are capable of. From a liberal humanist education to personalised learning in particular styles, and finally to a preoccupation with personal emotions, the collapse of belief in human potential is palpable.

Restoring Confidence by Example

The first step towards re-humanising education would be for educationalists to do defend a liberal education for all pupils in subjects such as literature and the arts, science, history and mathematics. The trouble is that they haven't the confidence to do it because they no longer believe children and young people are capable of education, which we've defined as meaning a liberal education. One answer to this lack of belief is to ask teachers to look at their pupils and students and see if they are more like James or another young person who we can call 'Alex':

> Alex is 15. She wants to study Maths, Physics, History and English Literature in the sixth-form. She is a voracious reader and wants to know everything about every subject. She is an accomplished musician and speaks French and Italian fluently. She writes short stories and has had one published. She is unsure whether she wants an academic career or to go into politics. Whichever she chooses she wants to go to the top, to be a Professor at Oxford or Cambridge or to be Prime Minister. She admires Mrs Thatcher. Her parents have no post-school education. Her mother works as a classroom assistant and her father works in a vehicle repair workshop.

Anyone who has been involved with the Institute of Ideas and Pfizer Debating Matters Competition, which involves students from a range of social backgrounds, will recognise young people like Alex, who describe themselves in such inspirational ways. Educationalists have a duty to humanity to offer all children the possibility of achieving what Alex had achieved by fifteen. To offer anything less is to fail ourselves, our children and humanity.

References

Anderson, J, 1980, 'Education and Practicality', in *Education and Inquiry*, Oxford: Basil Blackwell

Bookchin, M, 1995, *Re-Enchanting Humanity. A defense of the human spirit against anti-humanism, misanthropy, mysticism and primitivism* New York: Cassell

Claxton. G, 1999, *Wise Up. Learning to live the Learning Life*, Stafford: NetworkEducational Press Ltd.

Claxton, G, 2001, *A flying start on a learning Life: education for an age of uncertainty*, The Francis C. Scott Memorial Lecture given at the RSA on 7 November 2001. Available from the RSA website: http://www.rsa.org.uk.

Claxton, G, 2004, *Learning to learn: a key goal in a 21st century curriculum*, QCA: http://qca.org.uk/futures/

Coffield, F, Moseley, D, Hall, E and Ecclestone, K, 2004a, *Should we be using learning styles? What research has to say to practice*, London: LSDA.

Coffield, F, Moseley, D, Hall, E and Ecclestone, K, 2004b, *Learning Styles and Pedagogy in Post-16 Learning: A systematic and critical review*, London: LSDA

Cooper, D, 1993, 'Truth and Liberal Education', in Barrow, R & White, P (eds.) *Beyond Liberal Education: Essays in Honour of Paul H. Hirst*, London & New York: Routledge: 30-48.

Goleman, D, 1996, *Emotional Intelligence. Why it can matter more than IQ*. London: Bloomsbury

Hayes, D, 2005, Learning's too good for 'em, *TES FE Focus* 19 August 2005 http://www.tes.co.uk/search/story/?story_id=2124581

Hayward, G, Hodgson, A, Johnson, J, Oancea, A, Pring, R, Spours, K, Wilde, S, & Wright, S, 2005, *The Nuffield Review of 14-19 Education and Training Annual Report 2004-05*, Oxford: OUDES

Hirst, PH, 1973 (1965), 'Liberal Education and the Nature of Knowledge', in Peters, RS (Ed.) *The Philosophy of Education*, Oxford: Oxford University Press: 87-111

Hirst, PH, 1993, 'Education, Knowledge and Practices', in Barrow, R. & White, P. (eds.) *Beyond Liberal Education: Essays in Honour of Paul H. Hirst*, London & New York: Routledge

Johnson, M, 2004, *Personalised Learning – an Emperor's Outfit?* IPPR. http://www.ippr.org/research/index.php?project=233&current =23

Kant, I, 1978 (1781), *Critique of Pure Reason*, Translated by Kemp-Smith, N. London & Basingstoke: Macmillan.

Leadbeater, C, 2004, Learning about personalisation: how can we put it at the heart of the education system? DfES/Demos/NCSL: http://www.demos.co.uk/catalogue/aboutlearning/

Mill, J S, 1989 (1873), *Autobiography*, Harmondsworth: Penguin Books

NCSL, 2004, *Personalised Learning* (June 2004) http://www.ncsl.org.uk

Oakeshott, M, 1973 (1967) 'Learning and Teaching', in Peters, R. S. (Ed.) *The Concept of Education*, London: Routledge & Kegan Paul: 156-176

Pollard, A & James, M (eds.), 2004, *Personalised Learning. A Commentary by the Teaching and Learning Research Programme*, TLRP.

O'Hear, A, 1981, *Education, Society and Human Nature: An Introduction to the Philosophy of Education*, London & New York: Routledge.

Josie Appleton

Recentring Humanity

We need to move into a humanising period of history. This should come not in the form of a set doctrine, but in a new cultural and political sensibility. This is primarily a question of the starting point of thought and activity. What the humanising moment in history should decide is that the starting point for everything we do should be ourselves. Activity should be oriented towards human ends and goals, driven by human reason and creativity. After this period of history, it is possible that new political banners and allegiances will arise and this humanism of this sort will be needed no more: it will be the assumed framework for a new form of politics.

Alienated from our humanity

The reason this kind of humanism is needed is because we have become estranged from our humanity. Everywhere there is a discomfort with seeing things from a human point of view, or pursuing human interests. Indeed, it seems that we would rather see things from any point of view but our own, and defend any interests other than our own. This appears not as a craven attitude to the gods, but a craven attitude towards nature. While this remains the case, no form of politics can be possible, and every action or idea is merely a different form of running away from ourselves.

'Anthropocentrism' has become a dirty word, spat out along with 'humanocentrism', 'homocentrism' and 'humanism'. Indeed, apparently to see the world from a human point of view is 'speciesism', on a par with racism or sexism. Instead theorists hunt around for other loci of value:

'zoocentrism', 'ecocentrism', even 'cosmocentrism'. One author ponders that 'Rocks would have rights, on Mars', and concludes that 'humans ought to preserve projects of formed integrity wherever found' (Fogg, 2000). Animals, plants, even inanimate objects, are accorded with intrinsic value. One author argues that 'Naturocentric values are intrinsic, qualitative properties in nature. They are generated by animals (zoogenic value), by living beings (biogenic value), and by ecosystems (ecogenic value). Animals, plants, and ecosystems are able to generate values, thus being value-laden and not intrinsically barren of values' (Vilkka, 1997). She sees the point of human activity to discover other creatures forms of value — checking that they are independent of us — and to preserve them.

Intellectual work becomes a battle to strip away the humanity from one's analysis. Academics compete to find their locus of value as far away from humans as possible, something that one describes as 'ethical extensionism'. Thinkers pull each other up for allowing some human presumptions to slip into their work. One author holds up the animal rights philosopher Peter Singer for '[exhibiting] favouritism towards humans', because uses notions of consciousness and biography when evaluating moral value, and he also uses the term 'person' as distinct from animal (Fjellstrom, 2003). Another academic pulls up another by saying that their 'discussion of "human beings"…unnecessarily risks biology-linked issues of speciesism and sexism' (Wolf, 1995). The Turing Test is criticised for using human intelligence as the model for intelligence. Writers in the disciplines of sociology, cultural studies and literary theory have argued that the problem with their work is that they focus on the human point of view.

Uniquely human traits — consciousness, language, tool use — are seen as either useless or dangerous. 'What use is consciousness?', asks one writer in this area (Johnson, 1983). Others ask why we see symbolic language as higher than other animal forms of communication. 'Birds are able to earn a living and to raise a family outdoors without special aids or tools', notes one commentator approvingly (Barber,

1993), as if the human use of tools where somehow dishonest and estranging. Conscious activity, the very essence of our humanity, is merely seen as a violation of other objects' and organisms' 'formed integrity'. Human activity in general is associated with terms such as rape, conquest, domination, exploitation. All the finest virtues — courage, love, friendship — are only admired inasmuch as they can be identified in animals. The bookshelves grown under titles such as 'The Hidden Life of Dogs', 'The Human Nature of Birds', 'More Cunning than Man', 'Racoons are the Brightest People'. Communication is only admirable if it can be found in a species as distant from us as possible, such as an ant or a microbe.

Humanity has always — in different ways — experienced alienation from its abilities and desires. People have never been in full charge of their creativity; they have always shied away from the full use of their powers; and have always attributed events to forces outside of themselves. The task of expanding our powers and our understanding has been the work of history. But the alienation from our humanity is more intense and systematic than in the past. For example, Rousseau was ambivalent about human consciousness: he saw civilisation as a wrenching out of nature, a happy state where men had 'nothing to fear or hope' from one another (Rousseau, 1952). He notes that free will gives us a capacity for torment and for evil acts, as well as for achievements and good acts; where an animal is innocent, doing only what it has to do, man 'bring on fevers and death' by agonising over the results of his actions. As Luc Ferry puts it differently, 'Man is so free that he can die of freedom'. What we have now is not ambivalence about human consciousness, but a wholesale dismissal. It is seen purely as a burden, to be escaped in the greatest possible degree.

Today we don't fight against alienation, seeking to transcend it and achieve a fuller and more enriched existence. Instead we often experience it in a flat manner, without conflict or even much pain. The basis of tragedy — the thwarting of an individual's aims and desires by fate — is no longer with us, since we are flatly resigned to fate. One keynote work of contemporary pessimism, John Gray's *Straw Dogs* is almost comic. There is no point to human existence, he says; we are nothing, 'straw dogs', and that is that. There is no sense of 'the tragedy of unfulfilled aims', the sense of sadness that haunted the writer Thomas Hardy. Nor of TS Eliot's sense of loss, feeling that the 'glory of the positive hour' of culture had crumbled to dust.

Now there is little loss or hope: we have accepted our predicament with head bowed. In the much-celebrated novel *Atomised*, one of the characters finds peace in a coma, with the narrator concluding 'Perhaps the sun, the rain on our graves the / wind and the frost / Will end all our pain' (Houellebecq, 2001: 343). Transcendence in the novel is imagined only as creating a new sexless species, without the conflicts and dilemmas of humanity, and the book is narrated from the indifferent point of view of this species, which says of humans, 'we do not feel their joys, neither do we feel their suffering' (Houellebecq, 2001: 356). The scenario of aliens arriving from outer space is a narrative designed to express our contingency: *they will judge us*, it is assumed, and our standards and frameworks will be shown up for the flimsy things that they are. Scenarios are explored such as aliens arriving who value excellent eyesight above all else, and decide that cats are more sophisticated than humans; or aliens calling a 'convention of the Earth', and inviting humans as only one lot of delegates at the table.

Returning to our humanity

The task of politics now is to fight a battle against these many forms of estrangement from our humanity. It is about enlivening: breaking up the numb consensus that has formed, and celebrating the passion and conflict of human existence, even when that involves pain and doubt. It is about recentering: returning every question back to the ground of human aims and human desires. This will be a new starting point for a new chapter in history.

Those who will fight this battle will be those who are humanist in spirit, not just in name. Many of those who call themselves 'humanist' today are preoccupied with the threat from religion. But in some senses, religious people are more critical of contemporary culture's alienation from itself, than are those who call themselves humanists. Some Christians react instinctively react to the current attempt to locate all value and perspective in nature. For example, Richard Neuhaus, theologian and social critic, argued that 'the campaign against "speciesism" is a campaign against the singularity of human dignity and, therefore, of human responsibility' (Neuhaus, 1990). By contrast, a recent collection of humanism called on humanists to 'incorporate a substantive environmental ethic', in face of the 'anthropocentric preoccupations inherited from earlier centuries' (Seidman and Murphy, 2004). Meanwhile, the authors of a recent humanist manifesto sent a copy to Peter Singer to sign (who, incidentally, resides in a centre for human ethics). When humanists see anthropocentrism as a needless 'preoccupation', and appeal to animal rights activists for support, we have to question what that term means.

We need to draw inspiration from the renaissance humanist Pico Della Mirandola, and *start out from ourselves*. All thought and activity should start out from the point of human experience and our desires. In *Heptaplus*, he writes: 'We must go forth from ourselves, for the soul which does not see itself is not in itself. Whoever goes out of himself, however, is violently separated from himself' (Pico Della Mirandola, 1965). At present, people spend all their time trying to escape themselves — they would rather be anywhere but here, anyone but themselves, anything but human. They would rather speak for anyone or anything — for the unborn, for the Other, for the chimpanzee, for the moon rock — than for themselves as a human individual, trying to realise their ends and desires. But the ground of human experience is the only place from which intellectual work can begin. As the ethical theorist Susan Lufkin Krantz argued, without a rich concept of the human to reason about, 'reason simply goes its merry way, spinning out all manner of claims in the form, "because ... therefore ...', and nothing intervenes to check the process' (Krantz, 2002). Theorists go around attributing intrinsic value to this or that animal, but because they are speaking from the animal's perspective rather than their own, the whole process is entirely arbitrary.

It is *only in human eyes that things have one value* or another. That isn't to say that the human mind creates the laws of nature: nature exists apart from us, is indifferent to us, and follows its own laws. But it is only from a human perspective that these laws are made sense of or turned to any end. A mountain just is: it is only in human eyes that its many dimensions can be probed, seeing it as a source of raw materials, or as a place for recreation or artistic inspiration. As the French Enlightenment theorist Diderot wrote, if mankind were banished from the surface of the earth, 'the moving and sublime spectacle of nature would be nothing more than a scene of desolation and silence ... It is the presence of man which renders other beings interesting ...' (Davies, 1997). Nature produces no values of its own: all values are human. The attempt to attribute nature with values is merely a denial of our humanity.

The point of embarking on this new humanist quest is not to merely make our lives bearable. It is not to obtain a few crumbs of comfort, to live a life that is merely more *humane*. Sometimes humanism is presented as a kind of support network, seeking solace in the small pleasures of everyday life, from a nice meal to a conversation with a friend. 'All that survives of us is love' was the message gleaned by Martin Amis from the film *United 93*, a film that captured the doomed 9/11 passengers' last moments: 'love turns out to be the only part of us that is solid, as the world turns upside down and the screen goes black.' These small pleasures are an important part of living a full life, but they are not the be all and end all. We can offer more to each other than the touch and intimacy of love, as we face oblivion.

Human existence is contingent: there are no blueprints for how to be human. A tiger has no doubts about what it means to be a tiger, or how to use its claws: it just lives it and does it. We make ourselves; we decide our own terms. Pico Della Mirandola put this insight into the mouth of God, addressing man: 'The nature of all other beings is limited and constrained within the bounds of laws prescribed by Us. Thou, constrained by no limits, in accordance with thine own free will, in whose hand We have placed thee, shalt ordain for thyself the limits of thy nature ... the maker and moulder of thyself ...'. Today the contingency of human existence, the fact that we have a choice what we become, is experienced as scary — we feel as if we are on a plane hurtling through space, looking for a point of certainty. The touch and recognition of others is the only certainty we can find.

But what if, rather than fearing contingency, we celebrate it and start to explore its potential? We could start to look down at our own hands and think about all their many possibilities. Because these possibilities are *ours*, they are not so scary after all. People — especially young people — now are constantly looking for guarantees, trying to escape the dilemmas of existence. 'Where is it all going to end?', one 22-year-old asked me recently, worrying about the endless expansion of individuals' material desires. People now want guarantees, they want to know it's going to be okay and want to be assured of an endpoint. The idea of natural limits is a comforting thought, the idea that nature will provide a guide and not allow us to just 'do what we please'. We want to be subordinated to standards other than our own — to the values of chimpanzees or tigers, or to the needs of this or that ecosystem. The boundless, infinite quality of human desires is seen as too much to handle, so we try to escape that and take the standpoint of other organisms.

But that is because each person faces the abyss of contingency alone. If a group of people start to face up to the challenge together, and to start a debate about what life should be about and just what might be possible, then the openness of existence could come to seem exciting rather than a threat. As Marshall Berman has outlined (Berman, 1982), Goethe's Faust is an inspiration for the modern individual, with his cry:

> I feel the courage to plunge into the world,
> To bear all earthly grief, all earthly joy;
> To wrestle with the storm, to grapple and clinch,
> To enter the jaws of the shipwreck and never to flinch.

God is dead, but that doesn't mean saying that the point of life is merely to enjoy meals with a friend. Instead, it means that we ourselves take over the striving for perfection and for truth. Humanism should be looking for goals to leap for, rather than merely comforting us with what is.

The challenge is to start out again from ourselves: to see things through our own eyes, to reason from the ground of our own experience. This is only the start, but it could be the start of something very exciting.

References

Barber, Theodore Xenophon, 1993, *The Human Nature of Birds*, St Martin's Press

Berman, Marshall, 1982, *All That Is Solid Melts Into Air: The Experience of Modernity*, Simon and Schuster

Davies, Tony, 1997, *Humanism*, Routledge

Fjellstrom, Roger, 2003, 'Is Singer's Ethics Speciesist?' *Environmental Values*, Vol 12 No 1

Fogg, Martyn J, 2000, 'The Ethical Dimensions of Space Settlement', *Space Policy*, 16, 205-211

Houellebecq, Michel, 2001 (1998), *Atomised*, Vintage

Johnson, Edward, 1983, 'Life, death and animals', in Miller, Harlan B, and Williams William H (eds), *Ethics and animals*, Humana Press

Krantz, Susan Lufkin, 2002 *Refuting Peter Singer's Ethical Theory, The Importance of Human Dignity*, Praeger

Neuhaus, Richard John, 1990 'Animal Lib', *Christianity Today*, 18 June

Pico Della Mirandola, Giovanni, 1965 (1486)*On the Dignity of Man*, Bobbs-Merrill Company

Rousseau, Jean Jacques, 1952 (1754) 'Discourse on inequality', in Benton, William, *Great Books of the Western World, 38: Montesquieu, Rousseau* University of Chicago Press

Seidman, Barry F and Murphy, Neil J (eds), 2004, *Toward a New Political Humanism* Prometheus

Vilkka, Leena, 1997, *The Intrinsic Value of Nature*, Rodopi

Wolf, Susan, 1995, 'Martha C. Nussbaum: Human Capabilities, Female Human Beings', in *Women, Culture, and Development*, 1995, 105-116 (12)

Simon Blackburn

Humanism and the Transcendental

Poor old humanism comes in for some pretty strange attacks just at present. John Gray's wildly popular book *Straw Dogs* is perhaps the best known, although his target — if such a barrage of despairing scattershot could be said to have a target — was Utopianism rather than anything normally intended by the term 'humanism'. But there are two perennial doubts about humanism which do deserve a response. The first is the doubt that arises because humanism becomes allied in peoples' minds with 'materialism' and with the denial or downgrading of any spiritual dimension to human life, ethics, and politics. The second doubt arises because humanism is associated with 'relativism', or with a drifting, unprincipled way of life, incapable of sustaining real standards, real values and commitments. The first charge is that humanism is crass, and the second is that it is soggy.

The second charge has been rebutted sufficiently often in professional philosophy to deserve only a brief treatment. It does not take a 'transcendental' reality, the kind of thing accepted in popular religions, to underwrite commitments to values, obligations, rights and duties. The first problem with any such approach is epistemological. A reality lying beyond experience, beyond the here and now, beyond scientific investigation, might be a fine thing, if we could have any authoritative view of what it contains. But we don't. Wanderers into the hereafter paint different pictures. Gods come in all shapes and sizes, as well as no shape and size.

The moralities they are supposed to enforce are exactly as various as the human beings who claim a glimpse of them. In the eighteenth century the Christian God endorsed slavery and the death penalty for poaching; now he does neither. In Victorian times he disapproved of anaesthesia, today he disapproves of physician-assisted suicide, and tomorrow he will no doubt change his mind abut the second as he has about the first.

The other problem, less noticed than the epistemological one, is that whatever transcendental experience the adept professes to have undergone, he or she does not thereby escape the burden of judgement. Imagine a vision of one or another kind of a purported paradise or hell, and a promise that one kind of behaviour leads to one and another to the other. The adept has to use his or her judgement, first to categorise whatever was revealed as heavenly or hellish, second to estimate whether the promise is credible, and third to decide whether the threats and bribes that are supposed to modify his or her behaviour are such as would have been issued by a genuinely good authority, or merely by a capricious tyrant. A 'heaven' or paradise with 72 virgins for each man may appeal to some imaginations, but I hope not many, while a promise that you get there by random murder doesn't do much credit to its author. The Biblical story of Abraham and Isaac strays into this problem, but provides no resolution, except, of course, 'trust', or in other words leaving it to the religious leaders and religious traditions of the tribe.

Finally there is Hume's point, that the entire tradition of associating morality with any church inevitably distorts it, elevating the duties of observance and ritual above others, subtly or crudely demoting those outside the fold, ceding the power of judgement to persons with no earthly qualification for exercising it, and often more concerned to protect their own power and privilege than to do anything for poor old humanity.

On a more positive note, there is no need for transcendental sticks and carrots to underwrite morality. The fact that our moral natures are largely shaped by imagination, history, example, experience, and education, or in other words by the forces that make up what is vaguely indicated by 'culture', is not a source of shame. If things are going well, it should be a source of pride. We are not, by nature, all that nice an animal. It took time and effort, the work of persuasion and rhetoric, the goodwill of countless heroes, to get rid of capital punishment, slavery, the servile status of women, and no doubt many other horrors now concealed by time. Progress is not inevitable. We can go backwards as well as forwards. But that too is why a proper appreciation of the roads that have been travelled is so important. Without appreciating the directions that have been taken, there is no guarantee we will point the right way in the future, as the careers of those aficionados of religiosity, Blair and Bush, so aptly remind us.

So do humanists remain soggy? Why should we? There are boundaries to conduct, and we get hot under the collar when they are transgressed. These boundaries neither have nor need any supernatural source. Their source lies in our natures, our needs, our capacities for cooperative action, our sympathies and our concerns. There are behaviours and traits of character that dispose us to behaviours that are to be admired, and others that are to be shunned. Virtues and vices, duties and obligations, arise from the processes of meeting our own and others' needs in a setting of limited cooperation and allowed competition. I think we have not done too badly at that, although there is always room for improvement. Actually, I also think humanists can be a good deal less 'soggy' than anyone whose mind is half-fixed on an afterlife, or who has a head full of vague injunctions to ecumenicism, to universal forgiveness, to leaving judgement to God, and to turning the other cheek. Christians do manage to be fierce and resolute and unforgiving, but this shows only the limited power their own doctrines have when it comes to intractable human nature and human need. Of course, as suggested above, they are apt to be religiously intractable about other, more idiosyncratic things, such as heresy or apostasy or hankerings after the wrong kind of bishop.

The more interesting problem is that of 'spirituality'. Richard Dawkins has spoken eloquently of the awe and wonder he felt when gazing at the skulls of the earliest known hominids in Africa. The world opened by science is wonderful enough to arouse awe and fear or elation—the appropriate, complex, reactions to the sublime—in most of us. So we should resist the idea that there are special emotions available only to the adept, while only an impoverished 'materialistic' life is left for the rest of us.

Imagine two mothers taking a new-born baby into their arms. Each, we suppose, feels an overwhelming cocktail of emotions: relief, gratitude, pride, joy, love. Suppose one has a religion and the other does not. How is that supposed to give the one some kind of emotional high ground, a staircase up to some kind of rapture that the other cannot have? Suppose she finds herself thanking God or saying words of prayer. And the other thanks the doctors and nurses, and, equally literate, finds herself reciting words of Wordsworth or Blake. Is the former automatically deeper and more fitting than the latter? Is the latter 'materialistic' or 'unspiritual'? The idea is absurd. In one respect, at least, the secular emotional mix is more appropriate because at least the doctors and nurses get thanked, whereas when it is all down to divinity they may easily get overlooked. The secular mother can have her entire gaze fixed where it should be, on the new life in front of her, and is not even partly distracted by ghostly rivals for that attention.

Perhaps the leading myth of spirituality in the Western world is the drama of ascent from the cave, in book 7 of Plato's *Republic*. There are many things to say about the strange set-up, and the journey that Plato sketches. But there are at least two plausible alternative interpretations that compete with the usual idea of a spiritual ascent *away* from the world, and towards some kind of mystical illumination focused upon something otherworldly, or transcendental. Thus suppose someone says, alongside William Blake, that they hope: 'To see the world in a grain of sand, and to see heaven in a wild flower, hold infinity in the palm of your hands, and eternity in an hour', or even that they have managed to do so. One possibility is that their gaze has indeed been taken away from the sand, the flower, or the present, and has landed somewhere else, somewhere beyond experience and therefore transcendental. But the first alternative possibility — surely that which Blake was talking about — is that their gaze is still fixed on the grain of sand, the flower, and the present. Only now these are seen in the light of a wider context, perhaps even a timeless one. They are seen as one grain or flower or moment of time, but they are still seen for what they are. The attention is not divided, but rather in some sense infused with an imaginative sense of the wider spatial and temporal order of the world. This gives us a very different interpretation of what Plato was about. In the usual interpretation, the adept learns to turn his back on the world. In the alternative he learns to see the world but with an imaginative sense of its widest bounds. A second alternative, which actually seems to be the truest to Plato's own text, shares the view that attention stays fixed on the world. Only now it is the world seen through the lens of mathematics and science. The adepts of the *Republic* do not gain their illumination by prayer or meditation or fasting or self-laceration. They gain it by a prolonged education in mathematics and philosophy. They are theorists. They see eternity in the grain of sand in the same sense that a scientist might, who understands the laws of geology, or the physical forces holding the grain together, or the way different molecules combine in making up its structure. These forces and processes are in the relevant sense eternal. The particular grain of sand comes into being and goes out of being, but the laws governing its nature and its evolutions are forever. Or, if they are not, but have their own shelf lives, then their evolutions in turn would be understood only placing them in the context of equations governing other magnitudes and forces which outlive them.

Since this is so, Plato was kidnapped and traduced by the centuries of religious exploitation that take him to be elevating otherworldly concerns and states of mind above the mundane. His real concern was the priority of theory, and the place of fixed and unalterable natural laws in the scientific and mathematical understanding of nature. The path of wisdom is not to avert our gaze from nature, but to gaze at it properly.

So far I have accepted the usual contrast between humanism, as secular, and religion, as transcendental doctrine promoted by institutions. But that is itself a coarse contrast. First, there have been Christian humanists. And second, there have been persons describing themselves as religious, but who do not see their religion in terms of a set of doctrines, nor of allegiance to any particular institution. They may see it instead in what I should describe as aesthetic terms, that is, in terms of their wish to cultivate and experience a fitting reaction to our own mortality, to the lives of those who preceded us and those who will come after us, to the sublime and terrible moments of the passing show. They may think of their religion in terms of a set of practices designed to bring that kind of cultivation to the fore, as meditation is often supposed to do. They may, as it were, care more about church music than about theological doctrine, or syllogisms about substance and survival, identity and predestination. Ethically, they may care more about humanity or other sentient life, than they do about their own salvation, although those too may not be as separate as the cruder kinds of moral theory find them to be (there are currently flourishing industries of assimilating Kantian absolute principles, which are the kind of thing you lose your soul by transgressing, to the more quotidian injunctions and policies of utilitarianism).

Where these things are so, there is no need to fight about the labels. The real difference, it seems to me, is slightly different. On the one hand there are those of us who acknowledge that at the bottom lies nothing but our own judgement: human judgement, human emotions, human responses to the world and its problems. We need to take responsibility for our own judgement, where that includes our own attitudes and our own emotions, for those can be cultivated and can be misdirected, and can atrophy. On the other hand there are those who are happy to alienate their judgement, and let other authorities exercise it on their behalf.

In this division, what I have called the aesthetic attitude to religion is on the side of the angels. It is cultivating what Protestant divines used to call the inner candle of the Lord, or in other words the ability of the subject to respond and feel and think properly. From its point of view, there is no religion which is not intensely personal, any more than there is an appreciation of music with someone else's ears, or an appreciation of poetry in a language you do not speak. The religion of mere followers, the religion of the herd, is not religion at all but organised and dangerous delusion.

I am therefore quite shameless, as a humanist, about profiting from the best of our religious traditions. The poetry, music, architecture, and even, sometimes, the words are those of human beings struggling to express deep human emotions and feelings. They deserve respect, often. They may be better than any we would find for ourselves, unaided. But when we wonder whether they do indeed deserve this respect, there is no evading the burden of judgement. To think so blindly, to alienate our own judgement, strikes me as a kind of blasphemy, just as the subservience of reason to faith seemed to scholastics alarmed at the rise of Protestantism, and to any sane person watching the rise of American and Islamic fundamentalism.

If, as a humanist, I give this concession to an aesthetic religion, in an ideal world I would get the same back. But I am not holding my breath. Humanists can survive without fussing about their own identity or their own preeminence. A religious authority cannot: the whole institution depends on a claim to provide something better than anything that can be found without it. One of the more depressing tropes of Sunday newspaper piety is that atheism itself is a position of faith or a kind of religion of its own. It is not: there are many things from fairies to Norse Gods to flying saucers and astral influences about which we are all atheists. But we don't have a religion centred on a creed of denial of any of them. We just pass by, and wish people would change the subject, drop the vocabulary, concentrate upon the actual world, unmistakably present, immediate, and demanding as it is.

Bob Brecher

The Politics of Humanism

The secular gods appear to have failed. Communism is barely more than the fading memory of a twentieth-century aberration. Social democracy has been blown away, ceding the political space it once occupied to the neo-liberalism which it was always only its temporary role to ameliorate. Conservatism in its various guises was never in any condition to face down the postmodernity it rightly identified as its real enemy. The path trodden by so many — Hitchens, Kristol, Aaronovitch and the rest — from far left to neo-liberalism exemplifies today's realism about who we are and about what the world is like. There really is no alternative.

What is this neo-liberalism? In all but name it is the Calvinist version of Original Sin which dominates the fundamental thinking behind the dominant politics of today: and the leaders who pronounce on the masses are of course among the elect. Whether awaiting the imminent second coming of Jesus Christ in Jerusalem — the more apocalyptic American version — or working through an incoherent exceptionalism whereby those strong, successful, rich and ruthless enough to emerge as winners in the wars without end of the market will gain salvation — Blair's peculiar neo-liberal Christian fundamentalism — the message is the same. 'Ordinary' human beings are weak, frightened, inadequate beings who need to be protected from each other, at whatever cost. How they can also and at the same time function as the rampantly competitive individuals of the neo-liberal future might seem mysterious — until we remember that the conception of human nature at work here is seriously anti-egalitarian. The Christian fundamentalism of today's Anglophone neo-liberals has its roots in social Darwinism no less than in the Biblical traditions which biological determinism purports to undermine. But what is the idea of Original Sin if not a pre-Darwinian determinism? Not eating apples, but being born with certain genes; not a hubristic disobedience of God, but ignorance of biology: the rest is little different. No wonder, then, that their respective champions congregate on the battlefields of creationism, so-called Intelligent Design and neo-Darwinian biology. They mirror in today's culture wars the 'war on terror'. And like that so-called war between al-Bush and al-Qaeda, what makes those involved the enemies they are is the very closeness of their respective visions of the world, of the divine and of the human.

However mad those visions might be, however, they contain a vital lesson for the non-crusaders and non-jihadists among us — whether utopian ageing leftists who insist on distinguishing principle from realpolitik or younger people variously disgusted, disturbed, bored or amused by the inane 'realities' of today's politics and the 'common sense' of market commoditisation. The lesson is that there is something irreducible at stake here: the nature of human beings and the relation of that question to issues of what we should and should not do, that is to say, to both politics and ethics. For if we are not to join the Bushes, Blairs, Bin-Ladens and the rest in seeking salvation from the human condition through something outside us — some version of 'God' — then we have only two choices. We can simply give up on politics and morality, and thus in effect leave the world to market, mystical or some other non-human — and in all likelihood, inhuman — fundamentalist denial of the possibility of making the world a better place. Or we have to rely on ourselves to change the world, and to find within ourselves, as human beings, the resources we need to challenge and defeat the defeatists. In short, we need to remember Feuerbach's invocation of human possibility as what in fact constitutes the divine: 'God is nothing else than the nature of man purified' (Feuerbach, 1957: 180). But of course, we need to remember also Marx's earlier assessment of Feuerbach as insufficiently radical: 'The philosophers have only *interpreted* the world, in various ways; the point, however, is to *change* it' (Marx, 1975: 64). If we are to set about doing that, however, then we surely have to be able to know what it is that we are. Any form of humanism unable to identify the nature of the human which is the basis of that humanism would be laughable. The question of human nature will not go away.

I

But that raises an initial problem. Appeals to human nature as a means of justifying the status quo have always been a stock weapon of the powerful. 'It's human nature' has always been the refrain of those who sought to justify whatever it suited them to defend as part of the fabric of the world: war, slavery, serfdom, patriarchy, the family or whatever. Just as floods, earthquakes and pestilence were built in to the natural, physical, world, so these were built in to the constitution of human beings. And of course exactly this structure of argument is still with us: we are told that as human beings we are 'naturally' competitive, aggressive and egoistic, and that the structures and processes of capitalism thereby simply mirror 'human nature'. Nor is this sort of appeal to 'human nature' limited to just one side of 'debates' such as these. Utopians — whether Rousseau in the eighteenth century, Robert Owen in the nineteenth or the various Christian socialists of the twentieth — argue on the same basis: with the difference, of course, that they claim 'human nature' to be quite different, and to have been corrupted by civilization, industrialization or capitalism respectively. Prior to such corruption, human beings were co-operative, sociable and altruistic. Nor does it make any difference if the notion of what human nature is really like is projected into a possible future rather than onto a particular past. (Arguably neither Rousseau nor Owen were exactly clear which of these tacks they were taking; perhaps all forms of utopianism in fact combine the two, as the governing mythology of Christianity does quite explicitly.) The point is that it is political and moral conviction which determine what human nature is taken to be. No wonder, then, that appeals to human nature 'justify' whatever we wish them to justify, by simply and simplistically building the desired normative conclusion into the purportedly factual premise of the argument offered. So are arguments such as these not entirely useless? Should we not simply reject any appeal to human nature?

But if how we envision society has no basis in what human beings actually are — that is to say, in human nature — then on what other basis should we argue? What could possibly be the appeal, let alone the sense, of, say, a socialist vision of human relations which had nothing at all to do with what we are? Perhaps we should not reject such arguments quite so quickly, then. And we might start a reassessment by asking if it is the *structure* of arguments which appeal to human nature that is problematic, or the particular *content* of the premises invoked — that human nature is such-and-such — that constitutes the difficulty.

Might it be possible to delineate a notion of human nature on which people of different political and moral persuasions could agree? What sort of notion might fulfill such a requirement? Clearly, it would have to be a factual description, for otherwise we would be begging the question in just the way which we have seen to be problematic — their different normative persuasions would lead some people to reject a normative notion of human nature that others accept. But to the extent that a particular conception of what human beings are — of 'human nature' — is entirely non-normative, to that extent it is useless as a basis for normative conclusions. This is in fact the central difficulty for the most impressive attempt in the last twenty years to produce just such a theory, Doyal and Gough's *A Theory of Human Need* (1991), an attempt vitiated by its inevitably falling foul of the infamous 'Is/Ought Problem': one cannot derive a normative conclusion from purely factual premises. It does not follow from the fact that there is a child drowning in the river that you ought to do anything about it; it does not follow from the fact that human beings are aggressive in a purely biological sense — a purely factual sense — that aggressive policies and actions are not to be politically condemned (David Hume's is the classic statement of the problem, Hume 1969; see also Hudson, 1969). For the question always remains: given what *is* the case, what *should* we do about it? Should such-and-such a gene be eliminated from the human gene-pool? Given that she *does* not want to have a child, *should* she be able to have an abortion? No wonder, then, that John Stuart Mill tried to achieve a rather wonderful sleight of hand, by arguing that the only evidence we can bring to bear that something is desirable or acceptable, is that people as a matter of fact desire or accept it (as discussed by Mary Warnock; Mill, 1962: 26).

And there is the problem. What is needed is an unarguable yet normative notion of human nature.

II

It is in light of these considerations that I want to reflect on Frank Furedi's claim, central to his urging of a 'pre-political' humanism, that 'How we view the human species constitutes the point of departure for any philosophical or political orientation towards the world' (Furedi, 2005: 94). He is right in so far as his claim describes any already normatively committed conception of the human species: of ourselves as, for example, the creation of a god; or as a species really just the same as other species inasmuch as our behaviour is no less biologically determined than that of, for example, starlings. For the former, and whether or not they are prepared to admit it, what we do is not something we really *do* at all, since it is god who is in charge. For the latter, and again whether or not they are prepared to admit it, what we do is also not something we really *do* at all, since if biology (or anything else) determines what we 'do', then we cannot in fact be acting, but only behaving. And in both cases, what we are — whether children of god or purely bio-

logical organisms – is the starting-point, and indeed the fin-
ishing-point, of our thinking about what to do, or rather
'do', in the world. But Furedi's claim can also be misleading,
inasmuch as it is no less the case that our philosophical or
political orientation towards the world is the point of departure for how we view the human species. For those who are
not already normatively committed in some such way as I
have suggested above – to a god, or to biology – their philosophical, political and moral views about what we should
do in the world will play an important role in how they view
the human species. The two issues cannot be simply separated out in the way Furedi suggests. For unless we *already*
have a pre-existent non- or anti-humanist commitment, the
movement is from our philosophical/political commitment
to our view of human nature. And of course, that is precisely what the call for a *pre-political* humanism appears to
oppose.

The question then is this. In what sense, exactly, might a
humanism – a commitment to humanity and a confidence
in humanity's capacity to improve its state – be 'pre-political'? No humanism can be founded on some purely factual
conception of what human beings are, since in that case no
normative recommendations could be drawn from that
conception. Nothing would follow from such a conception,
as we have seen. But then if 'pre-political' cannot be understood as 'non-normative', how is it to be understood? What
other normative conception than a political one of what
human beings are could there be? Precisely to the extent
that we have a conception of our species at all, we are a political species, as Aristotle insisted when he remarked that we
are a political animal. If 'how we view the human species' is
already and unavoidably as consisting of political beings,
then our view cannot be pre-political at all. It must already
have some particular political content – for to say that we
are political beings but of no particular political character
would be an empty remark. To distinguish, for example,
between 'human being' and 'person' – between ourselves
as members of a specific biological species and ourselves as
moral and political beings – is to imply a notion of people as

some sort of moral-political beings, even if that sort remains (as yet) unspecified. So if by a 'pre-political' humanism is intended a humanism which is *non*-political, then it cannot be a humanism at all. For, to reiterate, from a non-normative conception of the human, nothing follows and no human*ism* is possible; and what normative conception of the human could there be which was not already political? Humanism, after all, suggests that there are qualities that human beings have — not, note, that there are simple facts about human beings — which have political and moral implications, and from which conclusions may be drawn about what to do in the world.

Historically, of course, to the extent that humanism arose in the West in opposition to Christianity, it has taken a broadly progressive politically character. To argue that we should put our faith in, and take our cue from, our own nature as human beings was to have already adopted a view of that nature that was, to put it crudely, benign and optimistic; the human qualities which were to constitute the basis of a normative system were understood in contrast to a conception of human beings as fallen, as beyond redemption by their own efforts and on the basis of their own nature. For otherwise, of course, what would have been the attraction of humanism as against Christianity? But, first, there is no conceptual reason why a quite different conception of the nature of human beings should not form the basis of a system of beliefs that takes its cue from that nature: consider the sort of humanism that might, and to some extent actually does, arise from contemporary sociobiology or evolutionary psychology. Second, and more importantly, a humanism of the latter sort would be no less political than the actual humanism of recent Western history. For again, to talk of 'the human' at all as something not purely biological — to the extent that normative conclusions may be drawn from such a conception at all — is already to invoke a political conception, both formally ('the human' is taken as a political, and not just a biological, notion) and in terms of specific content (what it is to be human is taken to be this and not that).

III

Unless, therefore, the notion of a 'pre-political' humanism is intended and understood — and both of these are important — as signalling something like a rejection of being bound by contemporary political formations, concerns and so on, it is hard to see what might be meant. However, if describing humanism as 'pre-political' were indeed just a tactic to do that, rather than to articulate and promulgate a principle which was 'pre-political' in some deeper sense, then I am doubtful how successful such a tactic might be. Such a humanism would be very likely indeed to be misinterpreted as 'non-political' and hence rejected — and rightly so, under that description. If we are to invent a humanism with teeth — some form of humanism has been going for centuries, after all; and its current form is politically marginal (a Feuerbachian humanism, one might say, rather than a Marxist one) — we need precisely to do the political work, intellectual and otherwise, of creating a particular 'political animal'. We need, not a pre-political humanism, but on the contrary an overtly political humanism.

Whatever the limitations of a political language which is a reflection of — as well as contributing to — the political poverty of our current situation, we need rather to invoke the continuing realities which the absence of an adequate public political language masks and to the denial of which it thus contributes so much. Socialism is not dead. Certainly its convictions and ideals have suffered political defeat; but that is not to say that those convictions and ideals therefore have no purchase and no worth. Furthermore, to accept linguistic defeat — even as a tactic intended to afford protection for the underlying content in a hostile world — would be no small contribution to ensuring that today's political defeat becomes the historical defeat that it has not yet become.

We need to think, not in terms of decades, but in terms of centuries. However ironically, we need to learn this much from the very religious tradition which humanism originally rose to oppose, namely Christianity. The choice is what it always has been, whether a hundred years ago or centuries ago, before the terms themselves had been invented: socialism or barbarism. If we as human beings are not the weak, frightened and inadequate beings today's politicians would have us be, then we should not be scared of asserting what needs to be asserted. A socialist humanism is no less apt today, and no less needed, than ever it was. Nothing less will defeat the defeatists.

References

Doyal, L and Gough, I, 1991, *A Theory of Human Need*, Basingstoke: Macmillan

Feuerbach, Ludwig, 1957 (1854), *The Essence of* Christianity, New York: Harper and Row

Furedi, Frank, 2005, *The Politics of Fear*, London: Continuum

Hume, David, 1969 (1740), *Treatise of Human Nature*, Harmondsworth: Penguin

Hudson, WD (ed), 1969, *The Is-Ought Question*, London: Macmillan

Marx, Karl, 1975 (1845) 'Theses on Feuerbach' (11th thesis), in Marx and Engels, *On Religion*, Moscow: Progress Publishers

Mill, JS, (Mary Warnock, ed.) 1962 (1863), *Utilitarianism* London: Fontana

Afterword

It would be premature to offer a conclusion to the debate on humanism following this short collection of essays. Rather it is to be hoped that the book will inspire further debate. Nonetheless, the essays shed light on several interesting and controversial aspects of humanism, and reveal more scope for debate even among those broadly sympathetic to humanism than might have been supposed. In particular, there is the disputed question of human nature and the possibility of universalism, transcendental or otherwise, and ultimately the question of what form a humanist politics might take. Some of the arguments made here can perhaps serve as reference points in this unfolding discussion. Many of the contributors are pursuing the themes explored here in their own work, and will be producing more in-depth books and articles on various aspects of humanism in the near future.

Without continuing debate and reflection, humanism cannot survive as a way of understanding and engaging with the world. Humanism can only flourish in a vibrant public sphere in which ideas are taken seriously and arguments forcefully made. It is a consciousness of this process, and a commitment to its development, that distinguishes humanist culture from mere media chatter. This is very much in the spirit both of the Societas series and of the Battle of Ideas festival. As I write, preparations are under way in earnest for the Institute of Ideas' second annual weekend of debate. Already we anticipate the third in late 2007 (www.battleofideas.co.uk), as an opportunity to build on the arguments made here and over the coming year.

The essays in this collection show that humanism is complicated thing, as full of potential for the future as it is rich in inheritance from the past. I hope that readers, whether or not they consider themselves card-carrying 'humanists', will be inspired to take the debate into the public sphere more generally, to develop and argue over the next step for humanism.

Dolan Cummings
Institute of Ideas
London
July 2006

Index

SOCIETAS: essays in political and cultural criticism

Public debate has been impoverished by two competing trends. On the one hand the trivialization of the media means that in-depth commentary has given way to the ten second soundbite. On the other hand the explosion of knowledge has increased specialization, and academic discourse is no longer comprehensible. As a result writing on politics and culture is either superficial or baffling.

This was not always so — especially for political debate. The high point of the English political pamphlet was the seventeenth century, when a number of small printer-publishers responded to the political ferment of the age with an outpouring of widely-accessible pamphlets and tracts. But in recent years the tradition of the political pamphlet has declined—with most publishers rejecting anything under 100,000 words. The result is that many a good idea ends up drowning in a sea of verbosity. However the introduction of the digital press makes it possible to re-create a more exciting age of publishing. *Societas* authors are all experts in their own field, but the essays are for a general audience. Each book can be read in an evening. The books are available retail at the price of £8.95/$17.90 each, or on bi-monthly subscription for only £5/$10. Details/updated schedule at **imprint-academic.com/societas**

IMPRINT ACADEMIC, PO Box 200, Exeter, EX5 5YX, UK
Tel: (0)1392 841600   Fax: (0)1392 841478   sandra@imprint.co.uk